THE NEW WORLD OF FAITH

THE NEW WORLD OF FAITH

AVERY DULLES, S.J.

Our Sunday Visitor Publishing Division
Our Sunday Visitor, Inc.
Huntington, Indiana 46750

Nihil Obstat: Francis J. McAree, S.T.D.
Censor Librorum

Imprimatur: ✠ Patrick J. Sheridan, D.D.
Vicar General, Archdiocese of New York
January 6, 2000

Our Sunday Visitor Publishing Division
Our Sunday Visitor, Inc.
200 Noll Plaza
Huntington, IN 46750

International Standard Book Number: 0-87973-692-5
Library of Congress Catalog Card Number: 00-130460

Cover design by Monica Haneline
PRINTED IN THE UNITED STATES OF AMERICA

Everyone who desires the baptism of Christ yearns for new life. Let him then leave behind what is old so that he may arrive at what is new. For in the past there was the old covenant, the old song, the old man. But now there is the new covenant and the new song, on account of the new man (cf. Eph 4:24). Let us explain what we mean with the witnesses of the Holy Scriptures. The prophet Jeremiah says, "The days are coming, says the Lord, when I will make a new covenant with the house of Judah" (Jer 31:31). Elsewhere, David the prophet says, "I will sing a new song to you, O God" (Ps 144:9), and also "Sing to the Lord a new song" (Ps 96:1). Likewise, the Apostle Paul says, "Stripping off the old man, put on the new" (cf. Col 3:9-10), and in another place, "The old things have passed away; behold, they have been made new" (2 Cor 5:17). What things have passed away? What things have been made new?

If a spiritual listener is present, he not only understands, but also sees what things have been made new.

— Quodvultdeus of Carthage, *The New Song*

Contents

Abbreviations

Abbreviations of books of the Bible are given according to the listing in the *Revised Standard Version, Oxford Annotated Edition*. That version has been used for all quotations from Scripture unless another version is indicated — namely, the *New American Bible with Revised New Testament* (NAB) in *The Catholic Study Bible* or the *King James Version* (KJV).

CA: John Paul II, Encyclical Letter *Centesimus annus* (1991).

DM: John Paul II, Encyclical Letter *Dives in misericordia* (1980).

DS: H. Denzinger and A. Schönmetzer, eds., *Enchiridion symbolorum, definitionum et declarationum de rebus fidei et morum*, 36th ed., Freiburg: Herder, 1976.

DV: Vatican II, Dogmatic Constitution on Divine Revelation, *Dei Verbum.*

GS: Vatican II, Pastoral Constitution on the Church in the Modern World, *Gaudium et spes.*

LG: Vatican II, Dogmatic Constitution on the Church, *Lumen gentium.*

SC: Vatican II, Constitution on the Liturgy, *Sacrosanctum concilium.*

SRS: John Paul II, Encyclical Letter *Sollicitudo rei socialis* (1987).

Introduction

In a recent apostolic letter (*Tertio millennio adveniente*, 1994, §36), Pope John Paul II has written: "It cannot be denied that for many Christians the spiritual life is passing through *a time of uncertainty* which affects not only their moral life but also their life of prayer and the *theological correctness of their faith.* Faith, already put to the test by the challenges of our times, is sometimes disoriented by erroneous theological views, the spread of which is abetted by the crisis of obedience vis-à-vis the Church's magisterium."

For some years I have had a growing conviction that believers, in a country like our own, are unsettled by the great plethora of ideas and options presented to them and by the allurements of instant satisfaction, which incline them to neglect the claims of eternal life. Yet they somehow sense within them that truth must be coherent, permanent, and universal. They long for communion with the transcendent and the divine. This communion is freely offered to us in Jesus Christ. We are called to acknowledge him and to experience the joy of totally giving ourselves to him in loving service.

In Christ, God opens up to us a new world of faith, in relation to which the world of daily experience is tired and old. The world of faith must be seen as a new and enduring order, which extends itself by the testimony of convinced believers. The times call for a more confident and knowledgeable assertion of the bedrock truths of faith. Some Christians are troubled in their faith because they make the world of common experience the measure of truth. They sometimes complain that the Church is "not up to the times," as though it had to be pursuing the latest theories and styles. It would be better to ask whether the world of nonbelief is still lagging far behind the revolutionary vision that Christ brought into our history.

These pages are written primarily for Christian believers and for inquirers into Christianity. They are written from a Roman Catholic perspective, by an author who came to Christianity and to the Catholic Church as a young adult. Everything in my life since that time has confirmed the rightness of that decision. I hope that as many as possible may share with me the joy and excitement of the adventure of faith.

In order to avoid getting lost in scholarly references and debates, I have tried to write this book as much as possible in my own name, without reference to the many authors to whose thinking I am indebted. My aim is to reach a relatively large audience that extends beyond the limited circle of professional theologians.

My impulse to write this work came from the persistent invitation of Mr. Gregory Erlandson, editor in chief of Our Sunday Visitor Publishing. He conceived the idea that this book should be written and asked me to try to write it. He has been very patient with my delays and has offered excellent advice for the revision of my first draft. Among the many other persons who have assisted in bringing this work to completion, I should mention especially my assistant, Dr. Anne-Marie Kirmse, O.P., who has given much sage counsel at every stage of the way; my editor, Mr. Henry O'Brien, of Our Sunday Visitor Publishing, who has supervised the editorial process; and Emily Cardozo, who assisted me with the index.

The Present Situation of Faith

Within recent memory there was a time when most people professed the religious faith in which they had been raised. Having received the faith through their parents, they could be counted on to transmit it, in turn, to their children. But this transmission of religious faith from generation to generation has become increasingly difficult. We live in a time of rapid change and fragmentation, reinforced by rampant individualism, which Robert Bellah and others describe as America's dominant cultural orientation. The sociologist Robert Wuthnow, in a book entitled *Loose Connections* (1998), speaks of "porous institutions." People move easily in and out of jobs, careers, marriages, political parties, and, of course, churches.

Present Obstacles to Faith

The present situation creates special difficulties for the transmission of a highly structured, traditional, and cosmopolitan faith such as Catholic Christianity. For purposes of illustration three impediments may here be mentioned: historical consciousness, pluralism, and the free-market mentality.

It is almost impossible not to be caught up in the historical consciousness that has emerged since the eighteenth century. We are acutely aware that the people of any given age have only limited access to the truth. Thanks to dramatic advances in science, many illusions from the past have been shattered. Deeply rooted convictions, taken for granted by our forebears, have been overturned.

Several examples readily come to mind. Until the seventeenth century, it was generally assumed that the earth stood at the center of the universe. But it has gradually become apparent that the earth is not the still point about which everything else revolves. Our planet rotates about the sun, which itself is by no means the center of the universe. In the seventeenth century, when the new astronomy asserted itself, many Christians, both Protestant and Catholic, considered that the geocentric view was a matter of faith. They even found passages in Scripture that seemed to presuppose that the sun revolved around the earth. But today that theory is universally rejected.

A second example is the application of historical criticism to the Scriptures. Until the middle of the nineteenth century it was easy to accept the creation stories in Genesis as literal accounts of the way the world came to be. But today most educated men and women in the world are convinced that the biblical creation narratives are largely mythological; that the world cannot have been created in the six days described in the Genesis, and that human beings probably descended from ape-like ancestors.

Historical criticism has made it very difficult to accept the literal accuracy of many biblical statements that earlier generations accepted without question. Stories such as the standing of the sun over Jericho and the survival of Jonah in the belly of the "great fish," which were sometimes taken as proofs of God's miraculous power, are today reinterpreted as poetic embellishment or edifying fiction.

These archaeological and scientific discoveries have an obviously negative impact on any Christian faith that is naïve or, as many express it, "fundamentalistic." Beyond this, historical consciousness can easily be turned into an argument for withholding any firm commitment of faith. Driven by the passion to be up to date, modern intellectuals adopt a critical posture to the past as a whole. As a consequence, even their present allegiances become tentative. Recalling that many venerable convictions of our ancestors have been shattered, they are understandably reluctant to commit themselves to any definite positions. Who knows what will be the next belief to fall beneath the relentless scythe of scientific criticism?

The second negative influence is the fact of pluralism. In the world of our day most people do not grow up in sheltered enclaves dominated by a single religion or a single set of social mores. They travel from place to place, and when at home they mingle with immigrants and visitors from other parts of the world. Intermarriage between people of different races, ethnic backgrounds, and religious affiliations is increasingly common. Through contemporary media of communication, we are thrust into contact with different clusters of ideas — religious, nonreligious, and even antireligious. It becomes obvious, therefore, that the faith of our own family and neighborhood is not self-evidently true. The realization that it is only one of many options makes any particular commitment more difficult if not weaker.

A third major source of difficulty, closely connected with pluralism, is the free market of ideas. In the realm of commerce new products are incessantly promoted by billboards, by mail, by television, and by the Internet. Our lives are caught up in cycles of production and consumption. Wordsworth's lament of almost two hundred years ago must also be our own: "Getting and spending, we lay waste our powers." Our attention is captured by new gadgets, amusements, and worldly satisfactions that would have eluded the most powerful and affluent monarchs of the past.

Many of us are so taken up with diet and food, sports

events, stylish clothes, new television sets, computers, and automobiles that little time is left over for consideration about the reasons why we exist at all. The pragmatic challenges of keeping our job, getting ahead in our profession, balancing our budget, maintaining our good health, and keeping up our family relations and social ties seem more pressing than seemingly impractical questions about God and religion.

In our pluralistic society the free-market mentality invades the sphere of ideas, including religious faith. Skilled recruiters, intent upon "church growth" and its secular analogues, are pressing us to join a multitude of vying movements and causes. Secular ideologies compete with religion, and the various religions are forced to compete among themselves. One possible result is the opinion that no one religion can be obligatory. The choice of a religion, like the choice of a brand of soup, is treated as a matter of individual taste. Religion is for people who are so inclined. If I happen to feel religious, I will buy into the religion that best suits my temperament. I will accept its tenets if I agree with them, and I will practice its rules as long as I find that they fulfill my spiritual needs.

The Persistence of Religion

Because of these three negative influences, and others that might no doubt be mentioned, religious faith ought by rights to be in decline. And in some places it is. But on the world scene the opposite appears to be the case. The great religions are enjoying a new lease on life. Hinduism in India, Buddhism in Southeast Asia, and Islam throughout the Middle East are flourishing. Christianity itself continues to expand, especially in parts of Asia and Africa. Notwithstanding the heavy inroads of secularism in Europe and North America, Christianity in these areas is experiencing dramatic renewals in small communities. The Roman Catholic Church, like some other groups, attracts a steady stream of converts. The prestige of the papacy was perhaps never so high. Pope John Paul II is widely regarded as the moral leader of the world. Here and there one hears predictions that the twenty-first century will witness a great resurgence of religious faith.

How can this be? A partial explanation, I believe, can be found in the human heart. We were not made for this world alone or for this life alone, but for something higher, which we can only glimpse. Spontaneously we reach out in hope and aspiration to the eternal and the divine. The sense of God is implanted very deep in our nature. Some would say that we know God instinctively.

Seen in the light of our consistent drive toward ultimate truth and meaning, the three lines of objection stated at the beginning of this chapter can be taken in stride.

Our first set of difficulties arises out of the recent growth of historical consciousness — the realization that the ideas of any one historical epoch are culturally limited. In itself, historical consciousness is a great asset. It has taught us that there is progress and development in the understanding of religious faith. But progress in religion, as in science, occurs cumulatively, through building on the past. It is not an excuse for historical relativism. If previous achievements could not be successfully transmitted from one generation to another, we would always be beginning again, so that progress would be impossible. Even in scientific "revolutions" the valid elements in previous theories must be preserved lest the innovation prove to be a regression.

There is such a thing as permanent truth. Every true proposition, in fact, is eternally true. The principle of contradiction (namely, that two contradictories cannot both be true in the same respect) is as valid today as when Aristotle stated it. Even historical facts, mutable though they be, enjoy a kind of permanence, in the sense that if they ever occurred they will never cease to have occurred. The facts that Plato wrote the *Republic* and that Brutus assassinated Caesar are abidingly true. So likewise, if it was ever true that God had a Son and that the Son was to redeem the world, these truths can never become false.

The rapidity of change may be seen as contributing to

the importance of finding out what is abidingly true. Confused by the continual shifting of fashions and opinions, we find even stronger motives to seek out the truth that is eternal. The impact of "future shock" deepens our attachment to unchanging truths about human nature and destiny, the moral law, and the divine. The great religions hold special attraction insofar as they put their adherents in communion with the eternal power that undergirds all worldly process — a power that revealed religion discloses as eminently personal. As a result, believers can pray, in the words of Henry F. Lyte's well-known hymn:

Change and decay in all around I see,
O Thou who changest not, abide with me.

With respect to Scripture, historical criticism has been an immense benefit. We know better than our ancestors that not every narrative was intended to be historical, and that even the "historical" sections of Scripture do not necessarily contain the kind of history that we would find in a modern academic textbook. Once this is recognized, we can better distinguish the various literary genres in Scripture, and gain a deeper appreciation of the legendary and poetic passages, with their powerful symbolism. The truth of the gospel can be transmitted by many means other than factual historical reports.

It would be foolish to fall into the trap of feeling bound to choose between science and faith. Since both are avenues to truth, they should be seen as allies. The same God who reveals himself in Christ is the author of human reason. God intends us to apply our intelligence to the data of faith. Every genuine advance in the realms of science and reason can be a positive contribution to the understanding of revelation. Nothing that science has established can contradict the truth of God's revealing word. Faith is not destroyed but refined and perfected by the exposure of the illusions that accompanied it when the disciplines of science and history were still in their infancy. Further fruits may be expected from an ongoing interdisciplinary dialogue in which each party must be prepared to learn from the other.

With regard to pluralism, our second source of difficulty, it may be said that the consciousness of having to choose among different options can make for a more personal and explicit faith, and thus for a firmer commitment. We may note in addition that religious pluralism is nothing new. Biblical history makes it evident that faith in the true God of Israel was always struggling against rival faiths and simple unbelief. Worshipers of Baal and worshipers of Yahweh contended against each other, often to the advantage of the former.

Christianity was born in a situation of religious pluralism and had to assert itself against formidable opposition not only from Judaism but also from a variety of Roman and Greek religions and philosophical systems. Many believers were martyred because of their faith. Christianity refused to settle for the religious relativism that had been practiced in the Empire. While confessing Jesus as the "one Lord," it had to face the objection that ultimate truth could not be a monopoly of any one religion. The pagan rhetorician Symmachus, in his controversy with St. Ambrose, protested that the pagan temples should not be closed by Christians. As his reason he stated that the mystery of the divine was so great that it could not be reached by one road only.

While we are not entitled to suppress other beliefs by violence, we cannot responsibly settle for skepticism or syncretism. It would be lazy or cowardly to decide that because people disagree, we should cease to struggle for the truth. Truth is one; error is multiple. Truth is self-consistent; error, incoherent. We have been equipped with minds to see the difference between truth and error, and to make a choice between them.

There may indeed be elements of truth in many different religions and ideologies. Let us by all means try to find and appropriate them. But we cannot appropriate anything unless we have the courage to name something as true. As we shall explain more fully in Chapter 8, interreligious dialogue can be profitable if those who engage in it are sincerely committed to different positions; but if the dialogue partners have no positions of their own, the discussion lacks interest.

The third line of objection calls attention to the distractions that preoccupy our minds and stand in the way of serious thinking about God and religion. The attractions of the senses have always been an impediment to religious commitment and fidelity. The Gospels are filled with warnings against letting the seed of God's word be "choked by the cares and pleasures of life" (Lk 8:14). Contemporary commercialism introduces no new problem; it simply takes advantage of weaknesses that have been present from time immemorial. Only a personal and explicit adherence to faith can protect us against being manipulated by persons who would play upon our weaknesses. To be wise, we must ponder on the origins, meaning, and goal of human existence.

The adoption of a faith, or adherence to the faith passed on to us, must, of course, be free. But if God is God, we cannot use him as a means of satisfying our whims. Our minds are made for truth, our wills for goodness, and our hearts for beauty. There can be no true fulfillment except in that which is really true, good, and beautiful. When we recognize it, it commands the full submission of our minds and wills. In this sense, religious affiliation can be obligatory.

What can reason accomplish in this area? A few centuries ago Christianity was confronted by militant rationalism. Philosophers were confident that reason alone could deduce all the really important truths of religion and morality from a few self-evident and indubitable axioms. They dismissed revelation as false or at least superfluous. But other philosophers, coming on the heels of the rationalists, punched holes in the alleged demonstrations, so that a wave of skepticism ensued. We still live in the shadow of this revolt against reason.

The great religions of the world have for the most part relied on revelation, but the majority of them, including Christianity, have not renounced the use of reason. Reason itself suggests the probability of revelation. If there is a God, and if he created the world, he will presumably interest himself in human affairs. People of nearly every race and culture have looked to God for help and salvation. The history of religion, therefore, cannot be adequately understood with the tools of psychology and sociology, as though God were inert or were a mere figment of human speculation. Knowing that God is real, we have to reckon with the likelihood that he might come to our aid and make himself known by revelation.

The religions of the Middle East and of the West are dominated by the conviction that God acts in history. Judaism, Christianity, and Islam agree in holding that God is one and is the lord of history; they believe, furthermore, that he is merciful and that he is pleased to come to the help of his needy creatures, especially those who turn to him in confidence. At privileged moments he breaks through the clouds of human ignorance and speaks to those who are prepared to listen to his voice. Faith arises not from merely human speculation but from attentive listening to the word of God, proclaimed by those whom God has chosen as his witnesses.

If God turns to us in revelation, we do not have the right to close our ears and to refuse assent. Our attitude should not be one of cold indifference or recalcitrance. On the contrary, the only appropriate attitude is one of eager expectation. It would be wrong simply to wait with folded arms, demanding that God should break down our resistance. If we listen to our hearts, we will often hear a gentle but persistent invitation to believe. In bringing us to faith, God draws us by the cords of love. If we are able to recognize a message as truly coming from God, we have no right to reject any part of it.

The New World of Faith

In the title of this book I maintain that Christian faith constitutes a new world. The gospel comes to us with the ring of novelty. Although in some respects it confirms what we might be able to know without it, it also tells of things we would never have suspected. As Paul wrote, quoting from Isaiah, God has disclosed "what no eye has seen, nor ear heard, nor the heart of man conceived" (1 Cor 2:9). Who would have imagined that God is three coequal persons, one of whom became incarnate and died for our redemption? The Jews regarded this as weakness, the Greeks as folly. But, to quote Paul again, "the foolishness of God is wiser than men, and the weakness of God is stronger than men" (1 Cor 1:25).

Newness is the very trademark of Christianity. It can never grow old. Christ establishes a new covenant. He makes us new creatures. He makes all things new, and will, at the end of time, usher in a new heaven and a new earth. Already by faith we inhabit this world that is in the making. We belong no longer to the old order, which is perishing, but to the new order that will be gloriously transformed in the final Kingdom.

To enter into this world is a decisive step. The transition is symbolized by baptism, in which we go down into the waters so as to die to sin, and we rise again to don the white vestments that symbolize the new life of grace. Baptism is a participation in the death and resurrection of Christ the Lord. The sacrament is not complete until it has been ratified by a personal confession of faith, accomplished with the help of the divine grace that is assured by the sacrament itself. But the force of the sacrament does not absolve us from the need of making the personal commitment of saying "Yes" to the gift that God offers us when we consent to die to sin in order to live by the strength of the risen Christ.

By baptism we commit ourselves to the following of Christ. We make his values our own. We accept the Cross and embrace it as an ensign of victory. This step is a revolutionary one, especially when we consider the dominant values of the secular world, including perhaps especially the world of our own day. To live virtuously for the love and service of God demands a conversion — a radical change, of course, from our habitual self-centeredness. All baptized Christians are called to be saints, that is to say, persons who have faithfully and consistently lived out their baptismal calling. Paul was able to say of himself: "Whatever gain I had, I counted as loss for the sake of Christ. Indeed I count everything as loss because of the surpassing worth of knowing Christ my Lord. For his sake I have suffered the loss of all things, and count them as refuse, in order that I may gain Christ and be found in him" (Phil 3:7-9).

To attain a pure and generous love of God we need more than our own natural powers. God elicits our love for him by first demonstrating his surpassing love for us. "In this is love," writes St. John, "not that we loved God but that he loved us and sent his Son to be the expiation for our sins" (1 Jn 4:10). Paul has a similar reflection: "While we were yet helpless, at the right time Christ died for the ungodly. Why, one will hardly die for a righteous man — though perhaps for a good man one will dare even to die. But God shows his love for us in that while we were yet sinners Christ died for us" (Rom 5:6-8). The Christian's love for God is an echo of God's prior gift of love.

Can we ever be truly at home in the new world of faith, so that it becomes not a realm that we ought to enter but our own world? This might not be possible if the call came only from outside us. But God gives us the Holy Spirit, the very Spirit of Christ himself. "God's love," writes Paul, "has been poured into our hearts by the Holy Spirit which has been given to us" (Rom 5:5). Elsewhere he points out the necessity of that gift: "The unspiritual man does not receive the gifts of the Spirit of God, for they are folly to him, and he is not able to understand them, because they are spiritually discerned" (1 Cor 2:14).

Paradoxically, we cannot find true happiness by seeking it for its own sake, but only by giving ourselves to what is worth all that we have. Jesus compares the Kingdom of God to a pearl of great price and a hidden treasure for which a merchant joyfully pays his entire fortune. In the light of the Spirit it becomes evident that the following of Christ is not impoverishment, slavery, or misery. Christ gives us inestimable riches, the fullness of truth, of wisdom, of beauty, and of love. He alone of all the human family could say of himself, "I am the way, and the truth, and the life" (Jn 14:6). His truth liberates us from the slavery of sin, from the fear of death, and from the darkness of ignorance about the true meaning of life. "Come unto me," he said, "and I will give you rest" (Mt 11:28). He does not compel us, but he invites us to embark on the glorious adventure of faith.

Christ's invitation still comes to all who wish to discover, or discover again, the inner joy of the Christian life. In order to meet the challenges of our time we must see the world of faith as a new and enduring order, established by God and capable of regenerating every human life and society. A vigorous and well-founded faith will not be constantly on the defensive. It will carry the gospel of Christ continually forward into areas where the darkness of skepticism and unbelief still reigns. Such a faith is conscious of being able to supply the divinely given remedy against the agnosticism, relativism, and hedonism that have always threatened to debase the human spirit, but are especially virulent in our own day for the reasons I have sought to explain.

2 Our Knowledge of God

Our age is marked by uncertainty about the meaning and purposes of life. Many do not know what to aim at, beyond the superficial goals of avoiding pain and "having a good time." But even while distracting themselves with amusements and sheer busy-ness, they can scarcely suppress their longing for a truth that endures and for a beauty that does not fade. In the depths of the human psyche is inscribed what some speak of as a nostalgia for God. On the part of reflective persons, this nostalgia gives rise to an earnest search. If God exists, he is to be loved, served, and adored in all that we do. But are there signs and evidences that God is more than a projection of the human mind? This pressing question can be answered because God has manifested himself in two different ways — directly by revelation and indirectly through the work of creation, as known to reason.

Teaching of the Bible and the Church

Religious believers rely primarily on revelation for their knowledge of God. They know that God is, and to some extent what he is, by entering into the new world that God fashions by revelatory words and deeds. He manifests his existence when he speaks to us and acts on our behalf. The prophets, the apostles, and the biblical writers pass on, with God's help, what they have learned from their experience of God's presence in history, especially in Jesus Christ. Just as a stranger can manifest his existence by shouting in the dark, so God can manifest himself by revelation and by the witnesses to his self-revelation.

Following Thomas Aquinas, the First Vatican Council taught that revelation is necessary both to know things about God that human reason could not discover by its own powers and also to enable people in general to know with ease, certitude, and without admixture of error those things about God that are in principle accessible to reason (DS 3005). Without God's direct self-manifestation in revelation, only a few people would know the one true God. That knowledge would require much time and effort and would not be free of error.

The Bible, as a preeminent repository of revelation, emphatically testifies, again and again, to the existence of the God whom we acknowledge in the creed as the "maker of heaven and earth and of all things visible and invisible." The God of biblical faith is omnipresent; he is so close to us that "in him we live and move and have our being" (Acts 17:28). In a very expressive passage the Psalmist can write:

> Whither shall I go from thy Spirit?
>   Or whither shall I flee from thy presence?
> If I ascend to heaven, thou art there!
>   If I make my bed in Sheol, thou art there!
> If I take the wings of the morning
>   and dwell in the uttermost parts of the sea,
> Even there thy right hand shall lead me,
>   and thy right hand shall hold me.
> If I say, "Let only darkness cover me,
>   and the light about me be night,"

Even the darkness is not dark to thee,
the night is as bright as the day,
for darkness is as light with thee.
— Ps 139:7-12

The biblical writers had a keen sense of the mystery of God. They were well aware that God is immeasurably beyond our comprehension. When Job tries to understand the workings of God's providence, he is confronted by his own incompetence. The Lord appears to him in a whirlwind and asks him, "Where were you when I laid the foundation of the earth?" (Job 38:4). For the next four chapters the Lord puts to Job a series of questions that reduces him to silence until at last he acknowledges that he has erred in trying to understand things too wonderful for him (see Job 42:3).

These considerations, far from justifying an attitude of skepticism or agnosticism, should bring us to reverent adoration. The Book of Sirach is especially helpful in this connection. After speaking of the beauty of the sun, the moon, and the stars, of the rainbow, the snow, and the seas, and the vast multitude of living creatures, the author concludes with a hymn of praise:

Though we speak much we cannot reach the end
and the sum of our words is: "He is the all."
Where shall we find strength to praise him?
For he is greater than all his works.
Terrible is the Lord and very great,
and marvelous is his power.
When you praise the Lord, exalt him as much as you can;
for he will surpass even that.
When you exalt him, put forth all your strength,
and do not grow weary, for you cannot praise him enough.
— Sir 43:27-30

Although the biblical authors rely on historical revelation rather than abstract reason for their own knowledge of God, they insist that God indirectly manifests himself in the work of creation, so that everyone, even without benefit of revelation, should be able to arrive at a certain awareness of God by reasoning from the things that are made. The author of the Book of Wisdom argues that the pagan idolaters are culpable because they ought to have learned from the beauty of the universe how much better is the Lord who created it:

> If through delight in the beauty of these things men assumed them to be gods, let them know how much better than these is their Lord, for the author of beauty created them. . . . For from the greatness and beauty of created things comes a corresponding perception of their Creator.
>
> — Wis 13:3-5

Paul may have had this passage in mind when he wrote in the first chapter of Romans: "What can be known about God is plain to them [the pagans], because God has shown it to them. Ever since the creation of the world his invisible nature, namely, his eternal power and deity, has been clearly perceived in the things that have been made. So they are without excuse" (Rom 1:19-20).

As this passage indicates, even our knowledge of God by reason depends upon God's prior revelation of himself through the work of creation. In a sermon reported in Acts, Paul speaks even more specifically: "In past generations," he says to the pagans of Lystra, ". . . he did not leave himself without witness, for he did good and gave you from heaven rains and fruitful seasons, satisfying your hearts with food and gladness" (Acts 14:16-17).

Our human knowledge of God, whether gained by reason or by revelation, or by some combination of the two, is always imperfect, because we cannot depict God except by comparison with inner-worldly objects, all of which are created, finite, and imperfect. According to the Fourth Lateran Council (1215), no likeness can be found between the Creator and the creature without there being a still greater unlikeness. But still there is a certain resemblance, because the Creator imprints something of his own perfection upon all that he creates. From the beauty and goodness of created things, therefore, we can infer something of the magnificence of the divine.

These reservations are important to keep us from falling into the presumption of which Job accused himself. We need to remind ourselves again and again that we cannot enter into the divine mind and look upon the world from God's point of view. We cannot understand how his eternal knowledge and volition relate to things that happen in time. When we speak of God's "foreknowledge" or "predestination" we are using misleading language, because there is no temporal priority in God's knowing and willing. His eternity is, so to speak, contemporary with all time.

The Fourth Lateran Council, spelling out certain biblical themes, authoritatively taught that God has certain attributes: that he is one, eternal, immense (unbounded), unchangeable, incomprehensible, almighty, and ineffable (DS 800). The negative form of many of these adjectives indicates the inevitable element of negation in our human grasp of the divine. We know better what God is not than what he is.

Building on the prior teaching of Lateran IV, Vatican I gives an even fuller description:

> There is only one God, true and living, Creator and Lord of heaven and earth, almighty, eternal, immense, incomprehensible, infinite in his intellect and in all perfection. As he is one unique and spiritual substance, entirely simple and unchangeable, we must proclaim him really and essentially distinct from the world, supremely blessed in himself and from himself, ineffably exalted above all things that exist or can be conceived besides him.
>
> — DS 3001

The Council goes on to declare that this one true God by his own free decision and omnipotent power created all things from nothing, and governs all things by his providence. Catholics, therefore, do not fashion their own idea of God according to their personal lights. They accept the teaching of the Church, which comes to them with the authority of God himself, and persevere in it unless they wish to separate themselves from the community of the faithful.

Spontaneous Knowledge of God

Belief in the reality of God is not restricted to people who read the Bible or accept the guidance of the Church. At least a vague awareness of God's existence seems to be almost universal. The majority of men and women proceed by a kind of spontaneous or instinctive knowledge, which teaches them that the world is not self-explanatory but that it depends on a higher Power. This latent sense of God's reality comes to expression in situations of danger, when people impulsively burst into prayer, invoking divine help. As the saying goes, "There are no atheists in foxholes."

Spontaneous belief in God can manifest itself when people are impelled to show their gratitude, amazement, or anger. When they escape from some danger, the words "Thank God" come to their lips. When they ardently hope for some future blessing, they say, "God willing!" They use — or misuse — God's name in imprecations and expletives. When they feel outraged, they call on God to punish evildoers.

In secular society, it is customary to invoke God in situations of particular solemnity. Rulers are sworn in by an oath of office, and witnesses in court are asked to call on God to corroborate their testimony. In every oath we bind ourselves and renounce the capacity for withdrawing from our commitment because we have made God the guarantor.

People of a reflective or philosophical turn of mind are not always satisfied by this vague awareness of God that wells up spontaneously in the human heart. They seek to translate it into rigorous arguments for God's existence. In the next few pages I shall summarize several arguments that have carried conviction for many serious thinkers throughout a number of centuries. These pages are intended not perhaps for every reader but for those with a taste for abstract reasoning.

Philosophical Proofs

The first of these arguments is taken from the fact of dependence. When we contemplate the world about us we become aware that all the objects of our experience, including our very selves, exist only because they are brought into being and maintained in being by external forces. Not only did we come to exist through the actions of others (our parents), but in order to survive we depend on a multiplicity of other existents — such as food, water, air, and sunlight. The question then arises: Can the whole of reality be made up of dependent beings like ourselves — things that exist not by their own intrinsic powers, but by the action of external causes? If A depends on B, and B is also dependent, there must be a C to account for the existence of B. But the chain of dependency cannot extend endlessly, or else there would be no sufficient reason why anything exists. To summarize the argument in more technical terms: There could be no contingent beings unless there were at least one self-sufficient Necessary Being, from whom all the others directly or indirectly derive their existence.

Objections are sometimes raised against this argument from dependence or contingency. Could it not be possible, some ask, for things to depend mutually on one another, like a house of cards in which the cards are supported by leaning against one another? Mutual support is certainly possible among things that already exist, but it cannot explain how things come into being. Only things that already exist can exercise influence on one another.

Equally pointless is the objection that there could be an infinite regress in causes and effects, each caused by its predecessor, so that no First Cause would be required. This would be like trying to explain a beautiful painting by saying that it was painted by an infinitely long brush. Since a finite brush could not even begin to produce the painting by itself, nothing is gained by adding length to the brush.

A simple example will perhaps be helpful at this point. A student can get a good mark by copying a paper from another student who got the right answers. That student, in turn, could have copied from a third. But it is absurd to argue that all the students were copying from other students, even in an infinite series. There must be at least one student who got the right answers by personal knowledge. A chain of dependent causes, even if infinitely long, does not explain the effect.

At first blush it might appear that the Necessary Being might be just a block of stone or a bar of metal, but hardly what people worship as God. Philosophers, aware of this difficulty, take the argument somewhat further. The Necessary Being, they argue, is utterly unlike the dependent beings we know from experience. It exists totally by its own power, as stone and metal do not. It must therefore have, or rather be, the absolute fullness of reality and power. From this one can infer that it has every positive perfection — every perfection that does not of itself bespeak limitation. Philosophers are able to demonstrate that the Necessary Being has life, intelligence, and freedom, and that it is therefore personal. The proofs are rigorous, but they presuppose a certain metaphysical aptitude and training that is not within the reach of every inquirer. One reason for revelation is precisely to make up for the weakness of the human intelligence.

This argument from dependence or contingency is only one of the many traditional ways for discovering the existence of God. A second argument, very popular throughout the centuries, has been the argument from design. When we look at the beauty of the natural world and contemplate the phenomenon of life, we are struck by wonder. How does it happen that sunsets are so beautiful and that flowers and butterflies are so elegant? How can one explain the facts that we have hands with which to grasp and feet with which to walk, that we have eyes to see with, and ears to hear with? Obviously we did not bestow these gifts on ourselves, nor can they be explained by any human agency. The human organism was not designed by any human architect. It must be the work of a wise and beneficent Mind.

The argument does not deny that natural selection could play a role in the development of higher forms of life. That which is unfit, no doubt, ceases to exist. But to account for the tendency of life to evolve to higher levels we need to postulate a purposiveness behind and within creation.

Sometimes people object to the argument from design by pointing to the presence of disorder in the world. Bad things happen either because people have bad will or because of the factor of chance. God has unquestionably created a universe in which people can violate his law and in which chance plays a role. In willing human beings to be free, God allows for the possibility of evil. In willing a world governed by physical laws, God provides for chance. Since what occurs by chance is disorder, chance does not require a disorderer. But order is not explained unless there is an orderer — one who adapts means to ends as the human eye is adapted for seeing. The fact that nature exhibits a notable degree of order is proof of Someone who ordered it. Ultimately, the argument leads us back to a supreme Orderer, ordered by no other. This can only be the Being we call God.

These metaphysical arguments, as I have already said, are dry and abstract. More humanly appealing is a third argument — that taken from the moral law or conscience. The sense of moral obligation seems to be a common property of all normal human beings. We experience ourselves as bound to do good and avoid evil. Some of our particular obligations are conditional, in the sense that we can be relieved of them by a change of situation or by an exemption from the law. But no one can exempt us from the fundamental obligation to do what is morally right and to refrain from doing what is morally wrong. That obligation is absolute.

How does it happen that we are under absolute obligations? There must be something above us, to which we are subject. We could not be bound by an abstraction of our own creation. A superior creature such as an angel could perhaps explain a conditional obligation, but only an absolute reality can account for an absolute obligation. Thus the argument from moral obligation leads to the conclusion that there is an absolute lawgiver, God.

This third argument can be rephrased as an argument from conscience, the "inner voice" that discloses the unconditional moral imperative. If we obey that voice, we have a good conscience; if we act against it, we have a bad conscience, a sense of guilt. Conscience gives us a realization that we are not our own masters. We are subject to a higher power and accountable to it. If I act against my conscience, I am amenable to judgment and punishment. For the moral life to make sense there must be just judgment, and this in turn implies a Judge who is righteous, holy, all-knowing, and all-powerful — in other words, God. These personal attributes converge with the metaphysical attributes discussed above, but they have a more "religious" quality because they imply an interpersonal relationship between God and human creatures.

A fourth approach to God's existence is from the restlessness of the human heart. We find in ourselves a great capacity to love, to worship, and to serve. We are constantly on the lookout for some reality, some Person, to whom we can dedicate our full energies and who commands our full devotion. Unless we find God, we are likely to idolize creatures and eventually be disillusioned. Either we must live with a void of meaning, which leaves us spiritually famished, or we must turn to God as the supreme object of our love.

The third and fourth of the preceding proofs are probably the most effective, by and large, because they are not purely theoretical. Our awareness of God comes about more through practical reason than through purely academic speculation. We adhere to God because we sense that otherwise our lives would be impoverished. We would not have the motivation we need to rise to our full human potentiality. To be our best selves, we have to accept the reality of God.

Need for Revelation

Only a minority consisting of highly reflective persons come to the conviction of God's existence from explicit arguments of the kind I have just been expounding. As stated above, most people accept the existence of God by a kind of wordless reasoning that is prephilosophical, or else because God has revealed himself by word and deed. Only those trained in philosophy are likely to formulate formal proofs, and even they will rarely be content with what philosophy can prove. They will feel a hunger to enter into some personal relationship with their Creator. Blaise Pascal, in a famous passage, pointed out that Christians adhere not to the God of the philosophers but to the God of Abraham, Isaac, and Jacob, the God of Jesus Christ. These are not, of course, two different gods but two different lines of approach to the same God.

Even if philosophy does not deceive us, it tells us too little, because it does not tell us about how God enters into loving communion with his people. This communion is something we desperately need. From the beginning of time, it would seem, people have been looking for indications that God comes to their aid, that he shows his love through mercy and forgiveness, and points out to them the path of salvation. Groping amid shadows, we cry out to God to give us light from above. Driven by our passions and desires, we turn to him for strength. By ourselves, we feel incapable of offering adequate reparation for our sins and restoring ourselves to God's friendship. Our religious instinct therefore impels us to look to God not only for truth and meaning but also for strength, forgiveness, and liberation. Revelation tells us not only about God's existence but about his fatherly care for us and his redemptive action on our behalf. In revealing his plan of salvation, God has unveiled something of his own inner mystery.

The Triune God

The doctrine of the Trinity is the point at which the God of Christian believers differs most markedly from the God of the philosophers. The Old Testament sometimes speaks of

God sending forth his Word and his Spirit, but it does not designate the Word and the Spirit as divine persons. In the New Testament Jesus gradually disclosed his own divine Sonship and at the very close of his life intimated the existence of the Holy Spirit as a third divine person. The discourses at the Last Supper, as reported in the Gospel of John, are particularly rich in this regard. Thus Jesus laid at least the groundwork for the Christian doctrine of the Trinity.

The New Testament, in a number of triadic passages, attests the Church's emerging Trinitarian faith. For instance, Paul at the end of his Second Letter to the Corinthians blesses them with the prayer that they may receive the grace of Christ, the love of God (the Father), and the fellowship of the Holy Spirit (2 Cor 13:14). The strongest of the triadic texts is the baptismal formula at the end of Matthew's Gospel. The apostles are sent forth to preach the gospel to all the nations, "baptizing them in the name of the Father and of the Son and of the Holy Spirit" (Mt 28:19). The implication seems to be that the three are coequal divine persons, though this is not explicitly stated.

In the early Church it was debated how the divinity of Jesus Christ and of the Holy Spirit could be reconciled with the monotheistic faith that Christianity had inherited from the Old Testament. There could be no question of repudiating the hard-won confession that there is only one true God. Did that imply that the Son and the Holy Spirit were less than divine? The Council of Nicaea (325) rejected the view that the Son was a creature, inferior to the Father, and half a century later the Council of Constantinople (381) condemned the idea that the Holy Spirit was a creature, subordinate to the other two divine persons. By the end of the fourth century, therefore, the doctrine of the Trinity was clearly in place. It was settled that the one God existed as three coequal divine persons, though certain fine points continued to be discussed in both the Eastern and the Western branches of the Church.

In 1215 the Fourth Lateran Council summarized in technical Scholastic language what we may call the developed doctrine of the Trinity in Western Christianity:

> We firmly believe and confess without reservation that there is only one true God. . . , the Father, the Son, and the Holy Spirit; three persons indeed but one essence, substance, or nature entirely simple. The Father is from no one, the Son is from the Father only, and the Holy Spirit equally from both. Without beginning, always and without end, the Father begets, the Son is born, and the Holy Spirit proceeds. They are of the same substance and fully equal, equally almighty and equally eternal.
>
> — DS 800

To speak coherently about the Trinity we have to stretch our human intelligence to the utmost limits. We find it very difficult to speak about God as he is in himself, for he is exalted far above all created realities and remains hidden from our view. Gradually, in the course of centuries, theologians worked out the category of "subsistent relations," which may be the best way of speaking of the divine persons, but this technical vocabulary presupposes an intense course of study.

The impression is sometimes given that because doctrines such as the Trinity so tax the comprehensive capacities of the human mind, they must be very difficult to believe. But it might to better to hold, on the contrary, that revelation would lack credibility if it told us only what we could figure out for ourselves. If God is the infinitely perfect spiritual Being, he ought to be mysterious to lowly creatures such as ourselves, whose knowledge is heavily dependent on the senses. If he reveals, God ought to be able to tell us things about himself that would not otherwise have entered into our minds. Paul had it right when he exclaimed: "O the depth of the riches and wisdom and knowledge of God! How unsearchable are his judgments and how inscrutable his ways! 'For who has known the mind of the Lord, or who has been his counselor?' " (Rom 11:33-34, quoting Is 40:13).

Difficult though it be to comprehend, the revelation of the Trinity is not useless. It enables us to realize that God's being is not static and sterile but dynamic and fruitful. Even within the divine nature, God is supremely communicative. He is a dynamo of spiritual activity. Since God is personal and spiritual, we human beings can best understand his inner activity by analogy with loving family relationships and with what we experience as thought and love.

The first person, the Father, is God in his primordial reality, the wellspring from whom all else proceeds. He is designated as Father in relation to the second person, the eternal Son, whom he begets from all eternity. All of us who have been brought into the body of Christ through baptism share in the Son's filial relationship to the Father, so that we may be called sons and daughters of God.

The Son is called the idea or Word inasmuch as he expresses the thought of the Father. He is the Truth that images forth all that the Father knows and has to say. He is the radiance of the Father's glory, his most beautiful reflection. If our ideas were as perfect as we might wish, they would embody all that we are and be persons like ourselves. In begetting the Son, the Father communicates to him everything that the Father has and is, except the quality of being Father.

The Holy Spirit, in turn, receives all that the Father and Son have, apart from their personal properties as Father and Son. He proceeds from the Father and the Son as their mutual love. If we wish to understand what love is at its absolute best, we will be drawn to contemplate the Holy Spirit, in whom divine love becomes a person. Such contemplation can be greatly assisted by participation in the prayer and hymnody of the Church, for example, the wonderful *Veni creator Spiritus*, translated into English as the familiar hymn "Come, Holy Ghost, Creator Blest."

The divinity of the Son and the Spirit is crucial for the doctrines of redemption and sanctification, which we shall be considering in the next two chapters. We are redeemed not by a demigod but by God himself, who enters into our history by the incarnation of the Son. We can marvel that when we were sinners God sent his own Son to be our Savior, and that "he so loved the world as to give his only-begotten Son" (Jn 3:16).

Equally astonishing is the good news that we are sanctified by the Holy Spirit, whom God pours forth into our hearts.

The spiritual life that grace opens up to us surpasses the whole range of creaturely existence; it is a participation in the inner life of God himself. As Peter tells us: We are "partakers in the divine nature" (2 Pt 1:4). The Son and the Holy Spirit are like the two hands with which God reaches down into the world to impart himself and bring us to himself. Through the inhabitation of the three divine persons, we are brought into the very life of God. He dwells in us and we in him. On earth we know this through faith, but in heaven the veils of faith will be removed and we shall gaze forever upon the truth that we now believe.

3 The Gift of the Redeemer

Original Sin

The world of grace to which we have access through the Incarnate Son and the Holy Spirit contrasts sharply with the world into which we are thrust by nature. The whole pattern of human experience and history attests to the power of evil. To a greater or lesser extent, all of us suffer from our own weakness and fragility and find ourselves victimized by the wild forces of nature and the brutality of our fellow human beings. Everywhere about us we see disorder, weakness, and decay.

We are, indeed, riddles to ourselves. In spite of our aspirations to holiness and to friendship with God, we yield repeatedly to temptation and fall into disobedience. We are, so to speak, in chains, enslaved by ignorance, suffering, and death. Our lower appetites rise up in rebellion against our reason and free will. As Paul wrote so memorably in his Letter to the Romans: "I do not understand my own actions. For I do not do what I want, but I do the very thing I hate. . . .

Wretched man that I am! Who will deliver me from this body of death?" (Rom 7:15, 24).

This pervasive disorder has social ramifications. We sense that all human beings ought to behave as members of a single loving family, but the actual situation is quite different. Individuals, clans, and nations are ranged against one another in a struggle for power, wealth, and prestige. They are caught up in cycles of vindictiveness that seem to have no end. The whole world, created for the honor and glory of God, has evidently fallen under the power of evil.

This paradoxical situation constitutes a theological problem and contains a hint of a theological answer. Although all things were created good by God, the divine plan has been crossed by some contrary design. Some original catastrophe must have destroyed the pristine harmony of creation and the integrity of human nature.

The Christian doctrine of original sin, partly based on the account in the third chapter of Genesis, has been developed retrospectively in the light of Christ the Redeemer. Knowing that Christ is the universal Savior, the Church infers that all human beings, and indeed the cosmos itself, stood in need of redemption. By his coming, Christ not only raises us to communion with God but also restores what was lost by the primeval Fall. The doctrine of the Fall mirrors in reverse the doctrine of Redemption. Just as one man, Jesus Christ, is the source of life and acquittal, so — Paul argues — one man, Adam, was the source of death and condemnation (cf. Rom 5:12).

Casting his vision even more broadly, Paul was able to discern that all creation is subject to futility and groans in travail, awaiting the Redeemer who would free it from bondage and decay. We ourselves are part of this picture. We groan inwardly as we wait for our full redemption and adoption as children and heirs of heavenly glory (Rom 8:14-25). This inarticulate longing is one of the mainsprings of religion. All peoples are sitting in darkness and the shadow of death. Without being able to express their need, they grope blindly toward Him whom the Church in its Advent liturgy describes as "the desire of the nations."

This universal human aspiration comes to its most perfect expression in the inspired literature of Israel. The descendants of Abraham, Isaac, and Jacob looked upon themselves as a people specially chosen by God to bring blessings upon the whole world, but much of their history seemed to contradict this lofty claim. They were repeatedly conquered by surrounding empires; their capital city was destroyed, and their Temple more than once desecrated; the people were deported to other lands. A succession of prophets, however, sustained the hope that the Lord would come to their aid; that their kingdom would be restored and that, under leadership of a "Messiah," they would be a light to all nations. There was much speculation about the priestly or royal features of the coming Messiah. Would he, as a warrior, bring all the nation's enemies into subjection?

Jesus as the Risen Christ

Jesus came into the world at a time and place of intense religious expectation, amid rumors that the Messiah was about to appear. John the Baptist warned the crowds who came to him in the Judean desert that the time of deliverance was at hand, but that the Messiah would come as a Judge and would spare only the righteous from his blazing wrath. The Gospels tell us that John recognized Jesus as the expected Messiah and sent some of own disciples to follow him. But he seems not to have foreseen the mildness and mercy that would characterize the ministry of Jesus. Jesus, when he came, overturned even the Baptist's expectations.

The process by which the disciples came to believe in Jesus is difficult to reconstruct because the Gospels, as we have them, were composed after Pentecost. They were written in the light of the Church's Easter faith and partly for the purpose of arousing faith. Thus they cannot be interpreted as strictly objective historical accounts of the sayings and deeds of Jesus and of the other characters they portray. Although they are in a true sense historical documents, the kind of history they embody is not the same as that to which we hold modern textbooks. The Gospels are more concerned with imparting the message and personal impact of Jesus than with capturing the details of what he said and did on this or that occasion.

For these reasons it seems advisable to concentrate, at least initially, on the conviction that the New Testament writers were intent upon instilling in their readers — that Jesus is the awaited Savior of the world, as the community of his disciples believed and proclaimed. The New Testament makes it undeniable that, several short years after the crucifixion, the disciples as a group were confidently heralding the news that Jesus was "Messiah and Lord," risen from the dead and enthroned at the right hand of the Father.

How do we account for the missionary proclamation of the apostolic community? It seems clear, first of all, that the missionaries were not preaching a deliberate lie. From the beginning they placed themselves in great danger of being persecuted, exiled, and even put to death because their tenets were considered blasphemous by religious Jews and subversive by imperial authorities. They would not have run such great risks in order to convince others to adopt a faith that they did not themselves believe.

The Gospel accounts, furthermore, cannot be written off as mere legend. They embody traditions about the words and deeds of Jesus that were carefully assembled by his disciples, some of whom were eyewitnesses. Apostles such as Peter, James, and John were authorities in the Jerusalem community, where the Gospel traditions were forged. The Evangelists consulted eyewitnesses and incorporated into their accounts key elements of the apostolic tradition, as we learn from their own testimony, from internal criticism, and from confirmatory evidence in other sources such as the Pauline letters.

While it was expected by many that the Messiah was about to appear, the expectation did not shape the picture of Jesus drawn for us in the Gospels. He was a very different type of Messiah than John the Baptist, the Pharisees, the Zealots, and others awaited. He disappointed their hopes and expectations by his humility, his reluctance to assume political power, his refusal of royal titles, and his repudiation of violence. His suffering and death on the Cross scandalized many of the Jews who might otherwise have followed him. After such an inglorious end, the disciples might well have despaired in Jesus except for an extraordinary occurrence that restored their confidence and transformed them into ardent witnesses. That event was, according to the unanimous testimony of all the sources we have, his bodily resurrection.

For the first Christians the Resurrection was not just a rumor or a theory. It was a fact that they accepted without the slightest shadow of doubt, either because they had personally encountered the risen Lord or because they were convinced by the united testimony of others who had seen him. This conviction motivated many of them to abandon their previous careers and devote themselves wholly to the worship and mission of the Church. Some of them became missionaries, eager to spread the Good News to the ends of the known world.

If the story of the Resurrection were told about some ordinary man or woman, it would no doubt be incredible. But it is told about a most extraordinary individual — one who worked unparalleled miracles, who taught with singular authority, who dared to correct the Law of Moses on certain points, who implicitly claimed equality with God, who identified himself with the coming Son of Man, and who superabundantly fulfilled many Old Testament types and prophecies.

This Jesus, moreover, stands at a unique juncture in the history of the world. Israel was approaching the end of the continuous history it had enjoyed since the time of Moses. In the view of the rabbis themselves, the prophecies and inspired literature of Judaism had already come to a close. The Temple, the very center of Israelite religion, was about to be destroyed. But a new age was dawning, in which the faith of Israel, fulfilled and transfigured, would burst forth from its chrysalis to become a world religion — one that to this day remains the largest and most geographically extensive that has ever been seen. The place of Jesus at the crossroads of world history is unique. It should not be surprising, therefore, that he might truly be a unique person, accredited by God in a most singular way, including bodily resurrection.

We cannot rigorously prove that Christianity is the true religion. Its acceptance is always, and necessarily, a matter of faith. We believe what God has revealed, relying as faith does on God's word. Our faith, though free, is not foolish or irresponsible. By the exercise of reason we can find signs pointing to the fact of Christian revelation. All the indications converge into a pattern, mutually confirming one another.

In the reflection of the early Church, the death and resurrection of Jesus was more than a sign confirming his testimony. As an integral part of the testimony itself, the Resurrection is inseparable from Jesus' own teaching about the path to salvation. It is a first installment of the coming Kingdom.

After he had risen from the dead, Jesus was able to convince the disciples that, contrary to their previous ideas, it was fitting for the Messiah to suffer and to die (cf. Lk 24:26). In his Passion he drank the bitter cup offered to him by his Father so that he might suitably atone for all the sins of the world. He became the Lamb of God, slain to redeem the flock, led meekly to the slaughter. Without this terrible humiliation he would not have become the Redeemer that he is.

Jesus heralds a new way of life, unknown in the pagan world and even in Judaism. Extolling sacrificial love, he teaches that suffering and death are to be accepted as elements belonging to the process of salvation. Believers are saved not *from* but *through* suffering and death. By baptism they are plunged into the death of Jesus and symbolically rise to share in his glorious life. Living out their baptismal consecration, they suffer willingly and participate through hope in the blessings of eternal life.

So revolutionary and far-reaching was the revelation entrusted to Jesus that he could not communicate it fully in his brief ministry on earth. If he had overtly claimed to be the divine Lord and Messiah, the Jews, and even his closest disciples, would have grossly misunderstood his meaning. He had to speak, therefore, with great reserve, often hinting rather than explicitly stating his self-understanding. His primary task was to prepare a small group of followers to be disposed to attain a better appreciation of his message after his death and resurrection. Thus we have his words at the Last Supper: "I have yet many things to say to you, but you cannot bear them now. When the Spirit of truth comes, he will guide you into all the truth" (Jn 16:12-13).

Dejected by the catastrophe of Jesus' condemnation and execution, the disciples were baffled by early reports of his empty tomb and reluctant to accept the holy women's tidings of his resurrection. Even when he appeared in person, they initially thought they were seeing a ghost. But he overcame their doubts by his continued presence in their midst, by his consoling and enlightening words, and by eating and drinking in their company. After he took his final departure, they confidently awaited the descent of the Spirit of truth whom he had promised.

The experience of Pentecost transformed the demoralized band of disciples into a unified apostolic body. According to the Book of Acts, Peter launched the process of evangelization immediately after Pentecost by confidently proclaiming to the Jews (including many pilgrims from the Diaspora) that the crucified victim was now reigning as Lord and "Christ." This last term (*Christos* in Greek) was here used not as a personal name but as a title, equivalent to the Hebrew "Messiah," the anointed one. According to the Book of Acts some three thousand hearers, from different parts of the world and different linguistic groups, were converted on that occasion — a striking sign of the destiny of the Church to include a vast multitude "from every nation, from all tribes and peoples and tongues" (Rev 7:9), gathering them into a single body.

The early Church was able to make sense of the rejection and crucifixion of Jesus by reference to the Jewish conception of expiatory sacrifice. According to the Gospels, Jesus spoke of his body being given and his blood poured out "for many" (Mk 10:45, 14:24; Mt 26:28). Paul declares that Jesus has redeemed us through "expiation by his blood" (Rom 3:25). Just as Moses had sealed the first covenant by pouring out the blood of goats and bulls, Jesus instituted the New Covenant by pouring out his own blood. The Letter to the Hebrews makes the point that the sacrifices of the Old Law were insufficient to purify the people from the guilt of sin. The Temple sacrifices were only types and figures of the true sacrifice of Jesus, who "entered once for all into the Holy Place, taking not the blood of goats and calves but his own blood, thus securing an eternal redemption" (Heb 9:12). The first letter of Peter expresses the same thought in unforgettable words: "You know that you were ransomed from the futile ways inherited from your fathers, not with perishable things such as silver and gold, but with the precious blood of Christ, like that of a lamb without blemish or spot" (1 Pt 1:18-19).

In the celebration of the Eucharist the early Christians recalled and experienced ever anew the redemptive power of Christ's sacrifice. They remembered his words and gestures at the Last Supper in words still used today in the eucharistic liturgy:

> The Lord Jesus on the night when he was betrayed took bread, and when he had given thanks, he broke it, and said, "This is my body which is for you. Do this in remembrance of me." In the same way also the cup, after supper, saying, "This cup is the new covenant in my blood. Do this, as often as you drink it, in remembrance of me."
>
> — 1 Cor 11:23-25

By partaking of the sacraments, especially the Eucharist, Christians of all generations affirm and perfect their identity as members of this covenant people.

Christ as God and Man

As we might expect, it took the community some time before they were able to answer the question about who Jesus was in precise theological language. After the Resurrection and the Ascension, the attention of the disciples focused on the lordship of Jesus now reigning at the right hand of the Father. Paul could therefore begin his salutation to the Christian community at Rome with a confession of faith in Jesus who was "descended from David according to the flesh" but was "designated [or, in the NAB translation: "established as"] Son of God in power according to the Spirit of holiness by his resurrection from the dead" (Rom 1:4). Paul's point seems to be that Jesus began to act powerfully for the salvation of his people after he entered into the glory of the Father. Paul is not here concerned with the more theoretical questions (which would inevitably arise in the course of time) regarding the divinity of Jesus prior to the Resurrection.

The early Church was excited by the realization that Jesus, as Son of Man, would return in glory to judge the world. Even before the birth of Jesus, Jewish apocalyptic circles depicted the exalted Son of Man coming "with the clouds of heaven" (Dn 7:13). Jesus at his trial before Caiaphas applied this prophecy to himself (Mt 26:64).

Although Jesus had repeatedly warned his disciples against trying to predict the time when he would return, many of them were convinced that this would occur within a generation. But this expectation was not fulfilled, and was difficult to reconcile with texts affirming that according to the plan of God the end would not come until the evangelization of the whole world had been completed (Mk 13:10). That task would require many centuries.

To overcome the disappointment of some believers, the New Testament reminds its readers that "with the Lord one day is as a thousand years, and a thousand years as one day" (2 Pt 3:8). Knowing that the Lord, at whatever time he comes, will not be late, the Church continues to look forward eagerly to his return. Meanwhile the leaders and members of the

Church settle for the prospect of a long sojourn here on earth, during which they will be obliged to transmit the faith from generation to generation.

Another facet of the mystery of Christ that gradually penetrated the Church's consciousness was his preexistence. A number of New Testament texts make it clear that before he took on human flesh, he already enjoyed divine life with the Father. The Gospels record numerous sayings in which Jesus mysteriously alludes to his prior life before he came into the world. Paul can say in the great Christological hymn from Philippians that before Jesus took on "the form of a servant, being born in the likeness of men," he existed "in the form of God" (Phil 2:6-7). The Letter to the Hebrews declares that God has spoken to us by his Son, through whom he created the world (Heb 1:2). The prologue of John's Gospel speaks of the eternal Word (*Logos*), without whom nothing had come into being, entering into the world and taking on flesh and dwelling among us (Jn 1:1, 2, 14).

Thus the Church in New Testament times confessed that Jesus was not only the Messiah and risen Lord but also the Son, the preexisting Logos, who had shared divine life from all eternity. The New Testament authors generally reserved the term God (*theos* or *ho theos*) to the Father, but in a few texts the Son is also called "God" (Jn 1:1, 20:28; Rom 9:5; Tit 2:13; Heb 1:8-9; 2 Pt 1:1). The realization of Christ's full divinity came to greater clarity through the prayer and worship of the community. From the beginning the disciples prayed to Jesus, even as they prayed to the Father. They baptized their converts in the name of Jesus, the Son, together with the Father and the Holy Spirit. They were convinced that the risen Lord, acting with the Father, had sent the Holy Spirit upon them.

Notwithstanding all these evidences of Jesus' divinity, there were some theological speculations that called it in question. Early in the fourth century, Arius, a priest from Alexandria, maintained that the Logos was inferior to the Father, the first of all creatures. This view, as we saw above in Chapter 2, was condemned by the Council of Nicaea (325), which asserted that there never was a time when the Son was non-existent. Far from being a creature, the Son exists eternally, one in being (or substance) with the Father (*homoousion to Patri*). This Council, confirmed by that of Constantinople in 381, authoritatively settled the question of the divinity of the Son.

In the fifth century the disputes revolved rather about the full humanity of Jesus. The Apollinarists (disciples of a bishop named Apollinarius) held that the divine Logos took the place of the rational soul (or "spirit") in Jesus. This idea was rejected by a local council of Alexandria in 362 on the ground that in that case Jesus could not be a perfect example for us, nor could he have redeemed our spiritual souls, which were in as much need of redemption as our bodies. The Fathers of the Church frequently appeal to the dictum "What was not assumed was not redeemed." Against recurrent tendencies to minimize the reality of Christ's humanity, and to treat it as a kind of disguise, the Church has continued to insist that Jesus is a true man, like us in all things except sin (cf. Heb 4:15).

The next question concerned the mode of union between the two natures of Christ. Nestorius, a bishop of Antioch, seems to have argued that the two natures of Christ were joined in a kind of accidental union, and thereby to have called into question the unity of the person of Christ. The Council of Ephesus in 431 condemned this view and deposed Nestorius from his see. It taught that the two natures of Christ were conjoined in the unity of a single person. This Christological dogma was filled out by the Council of Chalcedon in 451, which made it clear that even after the union, the two natures remained distinct, so that Jesus Christ was one person in two natures "without confusion or change, without division or separation" (DS 302). By this formula the Church rejected the heresy of the Monophysites, who held that the human nature of Christ was somehow changed and absorbed into the divine, so that it ceased to be a nature of the same kind as ours.

It was of the greatest importance for Christ to have a nature like ours, because he came to provide an example for us and to atone for our sins — tasks that required him to share fully in our humanity. It was also essential for him to be God, for otherwise he could not have taught with divine authority and acted with sovereign power on behalf of those whom he came to redeem. Because divinity and humanity were united in his very person, he was capable of reconciling the human family with God. By being united with him we are able to enter into the very life of the all-blessed Trinity.

At many points in its history the Church has had occasion to reassert against certain deviant tendencies that Christ is not just a human person intimately united with God. He is a divine person, God the Son. He could not possibly have fallen into sin, because it is absurd to think that God could be a sinner. Contemporary authors who try to make Christ more accessible by depicting him as a merely human person, or as one capable of sin, are simply reviving old heresies, rejected for good reasons many centuries ago.

The Purpose of the Incarnation

The New Testament teaches the fundamental purpose of the Incarnation: "Christ Jesus came into the world to save sinners" (1 Tim 1:15). In the Nicene-Constantinopolitan Creed, which we recite at Mass on Sundays and solemn feast days, we confess that Jesus became man "for us and for our salvation." In so doing, he did not simply restore what had been lost through sin. In the liturgy of Holy Saturday Adam's sin is called a "happy fault" because it prepared the way for so great a Redeemer. By uniting himself to human nature, the Son of God made it possible for all who received him to become, by a kind of "adoption," children of God.

Sometimes it is asked whether the Word would have become incarnate if Adam had not sinned. The answer to this hypothetical question is not given in revelation, but we may freely speculate. The Incarnation would surely have been possible because God's power does not depend on human sin. It would also have been, to all appearances, beneficial. Because one member of our human family is truly God, all of us belong in some sense to the family of God. The grace bestowed by the Incarnate Word surpassingly fulfills the highest potentialities of our nature. Through sharing in that grace, we are able to attain the life of perfect blessedness. Without the Incarnation, moreover, the universe would have been left without its crowning glory — that of personal union with the divine. For all these reasons it seems likely that the Son would have become incarnate even in the absence of original sin. But on this supposition Christ would not have had to suffer and die as he did. He would presumably have been recognized and welcomed by those to whom he came.

In the full perspectives of Scripture, the purpose of the Incarnation is much broader than we commonly suppose. Just as all things were made through the eternal Word, so his redemptive action reaches out to the whole of creation. Paul tells us that God has set forth in Christ his "plan for the fullness of time, to unite all things in him, things in heaven and things on earth" (Eph 1:10). The Greek verb here translated as "unite" means "recapitulate," in the sense of summing up and bringing to a head. Just as all creation, as we have noted, groans for deliverance from bondage and futility (Rom 8:20-22), so likewise all creation participates in the fruits of Christ's redemptive action. God was pleased, Paul writes, to make all fullness dwell in Christ, "and through him to reconcile to himself all things, whether on earth or in heaven, making peace by the blood of the cross" (Col 1:20).

In the light of faith, therefore, Christ assumes a truly universal role. He is the unifying principle of the cosmos, the source and norm of truth and morality, the consummation of all history, the goal and crown of all creation. As eternal Logos, he is truth itself, and as man he is the way that all must follow. Even the world of inanimate nature finds in him the source of its own power, order, and beauty and the principle of its own renewal.

As we seek to appropriate the Church's faith concerning

Christ, we shall find it helpful to immerse ourselves in the Church's liturgical prayer. At Vespers in the last week before Christmas the Liturgy of the Hours contains seven remarkable antiphons in which the Church takes upon itself the longing of Israel and of all creation for the promised Redeemer. The first of them, rather typical of the rest, reads: "O Wisdom, proceeding from the mouth of the Most High, reaching from end to end, ordering all things mightily and sweetly: come to teach us the way of prudence!" The antiphon for December 21, the day of the winter solstice, runs: "O radiant Dawn, splendor of eternal light and Sun of Justice: come and enlighten us who sit in darkness and the shadow of death!" By devoutly joining in prayers such as these we develop our capacity to profess, with God's grace, all that the Church believes and teaches concerning Christ the Lord.

Once Christ has come, he never really departs. If he seemed to go away at the Ascension, it was only to come among us in new form through the Holy Spirit. Therefore he can say: "I am with you always, to the close of the age" (Mt 28:20). By contemplating Christ we learn to understand ourselves in a new way, and glimpse how precious we are in the sight of God. Pope Paul VI, in his address to the Second Vatican Council of October 11, 1963, dwelt on Christ as our point of departure, the way we travel, and the goal we seek. He then called upon the Council to acknowledge him to be "the Incarnate Word, the Son of God and the Son of Man, the Redeemer of the world, the Hope of humanity and its supreme Master, the Good Shepherd, the Bread of Life, the High Priest and our Victim, the sole Mediator between God and man, the Savior of the world, the eternal King of ages."

These biblical titles afford material for endless meditation, giving joy to our hearts and light to our minds. We can never be grateful enough for the gift of the divine Redeemer. He stands at the very center of the new world of faith.

The Spirit and the Church

Although the Church did not begin to pulsate with life until Pentecost Sunday, its foundations had already been laid by Jesus in his public ministry and in his risen life. By gathering a band of chosen disciples, by selecting the Twelve and designating Peter as their head, by giving his followers forms of prayer and a body of teaching, and by instituting the Eucharist as a rite to be continued after his death, Jesus put in place many of the essentials. Then, in his risen life, he gave further instructions to the community of his disciples throughout a period of "forty days" (Acts 1:3). Before his Ascension he gave his final charge, commanded the disciples to go forth into the whole world, making disciples of all nations, baptizing them in the name of the triune God, and teaching them to observe his commandments (Mt 28:19; cf. Mk 16:15; Lk 24:47-48; Acts 1:8). On that occasion he promised to be with the apostolic leadership of his Church through all ages (Mt 28:20). He had previously assured the apostles that the Church, resting on the faith of Peter, would never succumb to the powers of death (Mt 16:18).

The Spirit as "Soul"

For the real work of the Church to begin, the sending of the Holy Spirit had to take place. After Jesus had returned to his Father's side he sent the Spirit "from the Father" (Jn 15:26). Pentecost may therefore be seen as the "birthday" of the Church, the moment when it began to possess an organic life of its own.

The Spirit was not at that moment becoming active in the world for the first time. He had been at work since the beginning. According to Holy Scripture, the Lord God created the world by his Word and his Spirit. "By the word of the Lord the heavens were made, and all their host by the breath of his mouth" (Ps 33:6). Since the Hebrew word for breath also means "spirit," this passage is interpreted as referring to the creative action of the Holy Spirit. The first chapter of Genesis speaks of the Spirit (or breath) of God moving over the waters (Gen 1:2).

In the creed we confess that the Holy Spirit spoke through the prophets of old. Prophecy, according to the Second Letter of Peter, comes only from persons moved by the Spirit of God (2 Pt 1:21). The Bible speaks of many pre-Christian prophets. The majority of them, such as Elijah and Isaiah, were Israelites, but some few, such as Balaam, belonged to other races. There is no reason why the Spirit cannot speak through people who are neither Jewish nor Christian, for as we know from the first chapter of the Book of Wisdom, "The Spirit of the Lord has filled the world" (Wis 1:7).

The Incarnation, in which the eternal Word of God took on our human nature, is from one point of view an accomplishment of the Holy Spirit, and indeed the Spirit's greatest accomplishment. Holy Scripture several times attributes this mighty deed to the Spirit. In the Annunciation to Mary the angel said, "The Holy Spirit will come upon you, and the power of the Most High will overshadow you. Therefore the child to be born will be called holy, the Son of God" (Lk 1:35). Joseph likewise was given the assurance: "That which is conceived in her [Mary] is of the Holy Spirit" (Mt 1:20). This teaching is echoed in the creeds. In the Apostles' Creed we confess: "He was conceived by the power of the Holy Spirit and born of the Virgin Mary." And in the Nicene-Constantinopolitan Creed we declare: "By the power of the Holy Spirit he became incarnate from the Virgin Mary."

The Holy Spirit dwelt in Jesus from his conception, but Jesus experienced new outpourings of the Spirit at various points in his life, such as his baptism in the Jordan, when the Spirit descended on him in the form of a dove (Lk 3:22). The Spirit led Jesus into the desert for his forty-day fast (Mk 1:12-13). At the beginning of his public ministry Jesus announced that the Spirit of the Lord had come upon him for preaching good news to the poor (Lk 4:18). He also claimed to be expelling demons by the power of the Holy Spirit (Mt 12:28). At the Last Supper he promised to send the Spirit upon the disciples to remind them of what he had taught, to make them his witnesses, and to guide them into the fullness of truth (Jn 14:26, 15:26, 16:13). Before his Ascension Jesus instructed the disciples to wait for the coming of the Spirit in power (Luke 24:49; Acts 1:4-5) — a promise that was to be fulfilled at Pentecost.

Both the Word and the Spirit are sent on their missions by the Father (although the Spirit is also sent by the Word). They have been described as God's two hands, but this does not mean that the Father does some things by the Word and others by the Spirit. The three divine persons always work in unison. The Spirit speaks only the Word of God, since he speaks only what he hears (Jn 16:13). Conversely, the Word is not effectively communicated except in the power of the Spirit, who makes it possible to confess that Jesus is Lord (1 Cor 12:3) and who confers the "grace of speech" upon those who proclaim the gospel of Christ.

Under different aspects the Church derives from both Christ and the Spirit. Christ is the visible principle from which the Church proceeds; the Spirit, the invisible principle. Christ, therefore, is often called the head of the Church, which is joined to him as his body. As visible head, he gives the Church its mission and its external form, its heritage of doctrine, sacraments, and apostolic ministry. But the Spirit, as the hidden source of the Church's vitality, is said to be the heart — or, more commonly, the soul — of the Church. He gives it life and vigor. According to Vatican II the Holy Spirit, "existing as one and the same being in the head and in the members, vivifies, unifies, and moves the whole body" (LG 7).

Since the Ascension of Christ the preeminent work of the Holy Spirit in our world is to guide and energize the Church. The Spirit dwells permanently in the Church as his home. But the Spirit, who resembles the wind that "blows where it wills" (Jn 3:8), cannot be confined within any fixed boundaries. In the history of ancient Israel, God raised up prophets and potentates from other nations to discipline or assist his people, and so likewise after Christ, the Christian community has no monopoly on the Spirit. The Spirit's activity outside the Church can be a grace for the Church itself. We cannot domesticate the Spirit, laying down rules as to how the Spirit ought to act. The most we can say is that the Spirit ordinarily acts in covenanted ways, through the sacraments and the instituted means of grace. He builds up the Body of Christ by distributing his gifts or charisms. Whatever is opposed to Christ and the Church is certainly not from the Spirit.

"Models" of the Church

As a supernatural reality, the Church cannot be neatly fitted into any human categories. It is a mystery of grace that must ceaselessly be explored without ever being fully comprehended. The most fruitful approach to the mystery is through images and metaphors. In Scripture and Christian tradition the Church is commonly designated by terms such as the Body of Christ, the Temple of the Holy Spirit, the People of God, the Flock of Christ, the Spouse of the Lamb, the New Israel, the new Jerusalem, and so forth. One distinguished scholar, Paul Minear, found no less than ninety-six images of the Church in the New Testament. Although any single metaphor could easily give a one-sided picture of the Church, all of them, taken together, tend to complement and balance one another.

In the modern period, until the middle of the twentieth century, Catholic scholars showed a marked preference for societal and political models of the Church. They viewed the Church as a kingdom or "perfect society" — perfect in the sense that it was equipped with all the means needed for accomplishing its mission. In so speaking they were not wrong. We ought never to forget that the Church is, under one aspect, an organized society. It has a body of official leaders who establish its doctrine, who perform its principal sacramental actions, and who are entitled to make laws and issue binding decrees.

As a visible society, the Church also has a determinate body of members, who enter it by faith and baptism. They remain in it by professing the Church's faith, by sharing its sacramental and communal life, and by acknowledging the authority of its pastors. Members who seriously violate their obligations are subject to various penalties prescribed by canon law. The most serious penalty, excommunication, administered only for grave offenses, deprives the member of the right to participate in the Church's sacramental life.

If we were to understand the Church only in societal and juridical terms, we would be seriously mistaken. In order to guard against this danger, Pius XII in 1943 issued a historic encyclical, *Mystici corporis*, proposing an ecclesiology based principally on the Pauline image of the Church as the Body of Christ. While he was careful to point out that the body is a visible and organized society, the pope insisted especially on a different aspect: the invisible union of the members with one another and with Christ, thanks to the abiding presence of the Holy Spirit. Unlike purely human societies, which are merely moral unions, the members of the Church are mystically united, inasmuch as the whole Church is animated by the Holy Spirit as "soul." But the analogy of the soul should not mislead us. Although vivified by the Spirit, the Church is not a single physical person. Having minds and wills of their own, the members continue to enjoy their own personal freedom and individuality. They are consequently capable of resisting the Spirit, committing sin, and even losing the faith.

Twenty years after *Mystici corporis*, Vatican II in its Constitution on the Church picked up the image of the body of Christ but supplemented it with a number of other images, notably that of the Church as the new People of God. In so doing, the Council intended to bring out the partial continuity between the Church of Christ and the synagogue, from which it sprang. Before the coming of Christ, Israel was already the People of God. As the new People of God, the Church may also be called the "new Israel" — a people not limited by any bonds of race or nationality but destined to be a lasting seed of unity for the whole human race (LG 9). As a sign and instrument of universal unity among all peoples, and of their communion with God, the Church may also be described as a sacrament of unity and of union with God (LG 1).

Images such as "People of God" and "family of God" have the advantage of bringing out the character of the Church as a communion of persons, a community. The supreme archetype for the Church is the divine Trinity, as a communion of persons intimately and inseparably united with one another. When Jesus established the "new covenant" in his blood, he brought his disciples into a deeply personal relationship with one another and with God. The Church, under one aspect, is a great family whose members are bound to one another with a love that derives from the Most Holy Trinity.

The term "People of God" should not be taken in a populist sense, as though it were an undifferentiated mob that decided on its own initiative to constitute itself as a society. As stated above, the Church's basic constitution was given to it by its divine Founder. The People of God therefore had a visible structure from its inception. From this divinely given foundation it develops its life and doctrine under the aegis of the Holy Spirit.

The members of the Church are all equal in their baptismal dignity, and all are alike called to holiness, to perfection. But for the health and vigor of the body it is important that there be different gifts and functions. To illustrate this, Paul compares the Church to the human body with its different members and organs. Just as the eye is not the ear, and the foot is not the hand, so the evangelist is not the administrator and the healer is not the prophet (1 Cor 12:4-31). Some are called to marriage; others to celibacy "for the sake of the kingdom of heaven" (Mt 19:12). Some are called to labor in priestly service in and for the Church; others are called to transform the earthly city by introducing into it the values of the gospel. Since all charisms are bestowed for service and for the common good, the members profit from one another's gifts. There should be no jealousy or rivalry among them. Each person should seek his or her personal vocation, cultivate it, and rejoice that others have other gifts. The greatest gift, that of love, is the common vocation of all members, no matter what their special role may be.

Many other metaphors could be studied to fill out our understanding of the Church. For instance, the Church is spoken of as the Bride of Christ, an expression that indicates the relationship of mutual love, care, and fidelity that exists between the Head and the members. And again, from a different perspective, the Church may be seen as the "mother" of the faithful. They are reborn and nurtured through the Church's ministrations, beginning with baptism, the fundamental sacrament of incorporation. As theologians have not been slow to notice, there is a radical difference between biological motherhood and the spiritual motherhood of the Church. The biological mother begets children by expelling them from her womb, but the Church begets them by receiving them into her bosom. We grow in the spiritual life by entering ever more deeply into the Church, the communion of love.

The Four Classical Attributes

In the creed we recite on Sundays and solemn feast days, we express our belief in the Church as "one, holy, catholic, and apostolic." These four adjectives summarize magnificently what the Church in some sense is, and always seeks to become more palpably. Just as a person may be a rational being without always acting rationally, or as a soldier may be courageous without always acting courageously, so the Church sometimes fails to manifest its true properties. The human persons who make up the Church are children of Adam, sometimes exhibiting more of their carnal descent than of their spiritual regeneration. They are capable of being deaf to the Spirit and resisting it. Yet it remains true that the Spirit is at work, seeking to build up the Church in each of these four aspects.

Unity means, in the first place, that, theologically speaking, there is only one Church. Christ has only one Flock, one Bride, one Mystical Body, one Temple in which he dwells. In the second place, it means that the members of the Church are united among themselves because all are united, through Christ, to the one triune God.

In any organism, unity is the result of a strong vital principle, or soul. As long as the soul is present, the cells and members of the body are united, but when the soul ceases to be present, as in death, the body disintegrates. So likewise in the Church, unity comes from the Holy Spirit who is, as we say in the Nicene-Constantinopolitan Creed, the "Lord and giver of life."

Because the members are not as much under the influence of the Spirit as they should be, there is always a measure of disunity in the Church. As long as history lasts, the realization of unity will be incomplete. The Spirit is constantly at work urging the members to overcome their mutual alienation and their schismatic tendencies. Anger, dissension, and rebellion come not from God but from the Evil One; where the Spirit reigns there is love, harmony, and peace (cf. Gal 5:19-23).

The second gift of the Holy Spirit to the Church is holiness. Conceived as he was by the power of the Holy Spirit, Jesus was called holy from the moment of his incarnation (cf.

Lk 1:35). At his birth the holiness of God entered definitively into the world. Consecrated at its inception by the descent of the Spirit upon it, the Church is by nature a holy Temple. It is holy in its faith, its sacraments, and its precepts. All its members, consecrated to the Lord by baptism, constitute what Scripture calls a royal priesthood, a holy nation (1 Pt 2:9).

The personal holiness of men and women is the true purpose of the Church. As Vatican II taught in its Constitution on the Liturgy, all the Church's activities are directed to the glory of God in Christ and the sanctification of the human family (SC 10). All the treasures of Scripture and doctrine, sacraments and sacramentals, ministries and charisms exist for this overarching purpose: to preserve the holiness that has been given, to restore the Church's pristine holiness, and to foster its growth in holiness until it measures up to the full stature of Christ its head (cf. Eph 4:13, 15).

The close connections between the Holy Spirit, the Church, and the sanctity of Christians is brought out in the Apostles' Creed, which says, "I believe in the Holy Spirit, the holy catholic Church, the communion of saints." The holy Catholic Church is constituted by the Holy Spirit and, through the mediation of the Church, gives rise to the communion of saints.

Sin is always an evil, because it is directly opposed to the will of God, but in the Church it takes on the added malice of being the profanation of God's Temple. According to the Letter to the Ephesians, sin grieves the Holy Spirit (Eph 4:30). It is a countersign that mars the true visage of the Church and gravely impairs its mission. All who have zeal for the sanctity of God's house will detest sin and seek to purify the Church by prayer, sacrifice, and penance. Without continually new effusions of the Spirit the Church cannot radiate, as it must, the holiness of God.

The third property of the Church is its catholicity, or universality, by which we mean its tendency and aptitude to spread everywhere and to take in everything that is naturally and humanly good. This attribute too comes from the Spirit. In any organism the soul not only unites the parts but also bestows a capacity for expansion. By virtue of our soul, our bodies are capable of assimilating food and our minds are capable of interacting with others, influencing them and assimilating what they have to give us. When people turn in upon themselves and stop giving to, and receiving from, others, they are in decline.

So too with the Church. When it fails to respond to the Spirit, the Church withdraws into its own sphere; its missionary dynamism becomes weak, and it loses contact with the world to which it was sent. But when the Church is fully itself, it interacts vigorously with the world, transforming it in the light of Christ, and assimilating and elevating everything that is good and pure. Cardinal Newman put this idea in memorable prose:

> As Adam gave names to the animals about him, so has the Church from the first looked round upon the earth, noting and visiting the doctrines she found there. She began in Chaldea, and then sojourned among the Canaanites, and went down into Egypt, and thence passed into Arabia, till she rested in her own land. Next she encountered the merchants of Tyre, and the wisdom of the East country, and the luxury of Sheba. Then she was carried away to Babylon, and wandered to the schools of Greece. And wherever she went, in trouble or in triumph, still she was a living spirit, the mind and voice of the Most High, "sitting in the midst of the doctors, both hearing them and asking them questions"; claiming to herself what they said rightly, correcting their errors, supplying their defects, completing their beginnings, expanding their surmises, and thus gradually by means of them enlarging the range and refining the sense of her own teaching.
>
> — *Essay on the Development of Christian Doctrine*, VIII.2.12

In more traditional language we may say that the Church takes to itself the abilities, resources, and customs of each people, purifying, strengthening, and ennobling all that it takes unto itself. In this way the Church gathers up humanity and all its riches as a pleasing gift to be laid at the feet of Christ the Lord (cf. LG 13).

The fourth and last property of the Church is its apostolicity. This means that it continues to be the same entity that Christ founded upon Peter and the apostles. Although the individual members of the Church constantly change, it remains the same society that was founded nearly two thousand years ago.

Apostolicity, like the other three properties, is attributed in a special way to the Holy Spirit. In any organism, the material elements are constantly changing, but its continuing identity is assured by the life-principle, the soul. Because I have a soul, I am the same person that I was twenty or fifty years ago, even though all the particles of my body have presumably changed.

Thanks to the Holy Spirit, the Church remains the same organized society throughout the centuries. Christians of our day have the same faith and the same hope that the apostles had, even though we may express it differently and see different implications. Just as a human person can grow in stature, wear different clothes, and change somewhat in appearance, so the Church expands and adapts itself to new and changing situations. The Spirit enables it to adapt and advance without losing its essential identity.

Accounting as he does for the apostolicity of the Church, the Spirit may be called the transcendent principle of tradition — the process by which the Church hands on the sacred deposit that was originally entrusted to its care. Tradition is often misunderstood as if it were simply the burden of a dead past, but it is far better understood as the "living past," the past that continues to be present. Whatever may be true in other areas, this is certainly true of the Church. Vivified by the Spirit of Pentecost, the deposit of faith continues to develop in the Church, pointing forward to the end-time when Christ will return in glory. Blaise Pascal wrote eloquently of the continual renewal of the Church in a letter of 1656:

> The truths of Christianity are certainly new things, but they must be renewed continually; for this newness, which cannot be displeasing to God, any more than the old man can please him, is different from earthly newness, in that the things of the world, however new they may be, grow old as they endure; whereas the new spirit continues to renew itself increasingly as it endures. "The old man perishes," says St. Paul, "and is renewed from day to day," and will only be perfectly new in eternity where the New Canticle, of which David speaks in the Psalm of Lauds, will be forever sung, that is to say, the song that springs from the new spirit of charity.
>
> — *Oeuvres complètes*, Paris, 1931, 3:451

The Church, existing as a human society within history, can always be studied with the tools of social science and secular historiography. These approaches, valid though they be in their own order, inevitably miss the inner reality of the Church, which is essentially a mystery — a reality imbued with the hidden presence of God. The believer, gazing on the Church with the eyes of faith, sees more deeply. In this perspective the Church belongs wholly to what we have been calling the "new world of faith." Animated by the Spirit of the risen Christ, it never ceases to relive the Paschal mystery of Christ's death and resurrection, to anticipate the final Kingdom toward which it tends, and to irradiate the world with the light of divine truth and the energy of divine love. The Christian life, and indeed human life itself, demands for its fullness a living association with the Church, which understands itself as "a lasting and sure seed of unity, hope, and salvation for the whole human race" (LG 9).

The Communion of Saints

In the Apostles' Creed we profess our faith in "the holy catholic Church, the communion of saints." Some theologians treat these two terms as synonyms, but historical study indicates that a distinction should be made. The term "Church" refers primarily to the visible assembly, with its apostolic heritage of faith, ministry, and sacraments. *"Communio sanctorum"* in Latin is ambiguous, since it can mean either "a participation in holy things" (that is, sacraments) or a "fellowship of holy persons" (that is, saints). The sacraments are not the Church, but they are structures whereby the Church actualizes itself and accomplishes its mission. The fellowship of persons, while not perfectly identical with the visible assembly, is its desired result, and will not be perfectly achieved except in the world to come.

The Church as Communion

In the documents of Vatican II, the term "communion" is generally used in a personalist sense, to designate the intersubjective relationships among fellow Christians. By baptism they constitute a supernatural community in which they enjoy one faith, one hope, and one common calling, sharing their gifts with one another, and seeking one another's good. Their common life is such that "if one member suffers, all suffer together; if one member is honored, all rejoice together" (1 Cor 12:26). The reciprocity of persons in the Church is a finite reflection of, and participation in, the fellowship among the three divine persons, who are perfectly united without detriment to their mutual distinctness and opposition. Communion in the theological sense belongs wholly to the new world of faith. It is a mysterious reality that could not exist except by the grace of Christ and the Holy Spirit.

The Church, according to Vatican II, is an effective sign, a "sacrament," of this wonderful network of interpersonal relationships. Although the Church tends to bring about this communion, it does so with varying degrees of success. Some who belong interiorly to the communion of saints are not formally incorporated into the Church, and some baptized and believing members of the Church, having fallen into sin, are excluded from the spiritual fellowship unless and until they repent and obtain forgiveness.

Communion in the Church is not simply interior and spiritual. In the Church as a visible society, there are structures of communion. Communion is more perfect to the extent that the members profess the same beliefs, celebrate the same sacraments, and recognize the same pastoral leaders. Communion is impaired or ruptured by failure to profess the Church's full faith, by abstention from its sacraments, by disobedience to its appointed pastors, and by schismatic withdrawal from association with the faithful members.

Baptism, the sacrament of regeneration, is the basic sacrament of communion. It visibly incorporates the recipient into the Body of Christ, which is the Church. Communion is realized most fully through the Eucharist, which enables the members to enter into a deeper union with Christ and his Body, inasmuch as all who partake of it are, as Paul expresses it, nourished by "the one bread" (1 Cor 10:17). Thomas Aquinas memorably called the Eucharist "the sacrament of ecclesiastical unity." Celebrated among those who are truly united in faith and fellowship, it both expresses and intensifies their communion with one another.

The bishops who are ordained to be teachers and pastors in the Church are united with one another in a relationship of mutual solidarity technically known as "hierarchical communion." Within this network of communion, the bishops develop a spirit of unity and solidarity, exchanging their insights and experiences, seeking to arrive at common judgments and harmonious policies. Hierarchical communion can be broken if a given bishop or group of bishops falls into heresy or schism.

The concept of communion also covers the relationships between the particular churches, of which the bishops are pastors. Vatican Council II did much to restore the ancient idea of the universal Church as a communion of particular churches, all of which live off their own particular traditions. It encouraged churches in different parts of the world to express and celebrate their faith differently, in accordance with the native gifts, talents, and traditions of the people. The pope, as successor of Peter, presides over the whole assembly, protecting legitimate differences and at the same time keeping those differences from becoming divisive.

The word "communion" therefore has several levels of meaning. It refers to the whole network of visible bonds among the faithful, their pastors, and their particular churches, but it also refers to the interior union of hearts and minds brought about by the indwelling of the same Holy Spirit in the whole Church and its individual members. When they speak of the "communion of saints," people today are generally referring to the interior, spiritual bonds joining the faithful to one another in God. This spiritual communion is the very goal of the Church, since its institutional structures were established for the salvation and sanctification of the members.

The communion of saints embraces all members of the body of Christ, whether on earth, in purgatory, or in heaven.

Bound together in supernatural solidarity, they can benefit one another by their holiness, which builds up the Church as a whole, and harm one another by their sins, which degrade the Church and diminish its salvific efficacy. Within the Body of Christ, we can all profit from the prayers of others and from their good works and sufferings, offered on our behalf.

With this realization, the practice developed in the early Church for penitents, while doing penance for their sins, to beg the community to offer prayers and sacrifices, especially the eucharistic sacrifice, on their behalf. Martyrs on the way to execution sometimes promised to offer their sufferings to God in reparation for the sins of penitents seeking reconciliation. The Church sometimes recognized such actions as substitutes for the performance of canonical penances.

These practices lie at the root of the doctrine of indulgences, which has developed over the centuries. Contrary to a widespread impression, an indulgence is not a remission of sin or guilt. It is defined as a remission of the temporal punishment due to sins whose guilt has already been forgiven. The Church specifies the conditions under which an indulgence can be gained — perhaps a pilgrimage, a work of charity, or the recitation of certain prayers, in addition to the basic requirements of sacramental confession and participation in the Eucharist. The recipient must not only perform the prescribed work but also love God, trust in Christ's merits, and believe in the help that can be obtained from the communion of saints.

The faithful can gain indulgences for themselves or apply them to the souls in purgatory, who are no longer in a position to make reparation for their sins. The Church does not have dominion over purgatory but trusts in God to alleviate the sufferings of the souls for whom the Church offers, in satisfaction, the good works performed and the sufferings endured by holy persons on earth. Indulgences, in this context, are official prayers of the Church that the merits of Christ and the saints be applied for the souls of the deceased undergoing purification.

The communion of saints exists most tangibly here on

earth, where the faithful help one another by instruction, advice, friendship, and material assistance. In the early centuries Christians traveling abroad were accustomed to bring with them "letters of communion" from their own bishops, entitling them to receive hospitality and be admitted to the worship of the community they were visiting. In the individualistic culture of our day, we should seek to recover this spirit of solidarity in Christ. Our bonds of communion in the Church know no limits of nationality, race, or language.

Holy Scripture helps us to overcome excessive individualism. Holiness never exists except in a social setting. The infancy accounts in the Gospels of Matthew and Luke make it clear that Jesus did not descend into the human situation like a meteor from the sky. In his humanity he had a physical and spiritual ancestry; he belonged to the family, nationality, and culture in which he was born and raised. Jesus, Mary, and Joseph were deeply inserted into a circle of humble and devout believers, including Zachary and Elizabeth, Simeon and Anna. John the Baptist could hardly have risen to such heights of holiness without having been raised in an environment of saintly persons. As a child, Jesus was nurtured in the faith and the religious life of Israel by his relatives and acquaintances. Taught by them, he expressed his relationship to God and his spiritual mission in terms derived from Old Testament type and prophecy.

In his public life, Jesus laid the foundations for a new communion more intimate than flesh and blood. "Whoever does the will of God," he said, "is my brother, and sister, and mother" (Mk 3:35). The condition of entry into this communion was holiness. Every member of his community was called upon to practice the beatitudes and to be perfect, even as his Father was perfect (Mt 5:48). The disciples were to be conspicuous by their mutual love and union (Jn 17:21-23).

The Saints

In apostolic times the members of the Church were known as saints, since they had been spiritually cleansed by the waters of baptism and were engaged in the quest for holiness. The Church was confident that Christ was at work in all the baptized, and that their union with him would not be dissolved by death.

Exemplary members of this community are known as "saints" in a stricter meaning of the term — men and women in whom the grace of God has been preeminently successful, and who serve as models of the Christian life. Only God can make saints, but it is the business of the Church to recognize and authenticate them, so that their example and teaching may be of greater benefit to others on their journey of faith. The process of canonization in the Catholic Church is long and complex. It normally requires extensive research and testimony about the beliefs, teaching, and life of the person in question. Miracles are required so that the authentication itself may come ultimately from God.

In the Middle Ages the cult of the saints became exuberant to the point of falling into excesses. A venal clergy, in combination with a gullible and largely illiterate populace, furnished a breeding ground for fanciful legends about apparitions, heavenly messages, and miraculous cures. The barriers between this world and the next seemed tenuous indeed. The fires of hell and purgatory were vividly imagined. Indulgences, pilgrimages, relics, and votive Masses became objects of a thriving business.

Reacting against these abuses, the Protestant Reformers went to the opposite extreme. They expressed doubts about the intercession of the saints and discouraged the practice of invoking their intercession on the ground that it detracted from reliance on "Christ alone." Commemorations of the saints were excised from the liturgy. In some Reformed churches masterpieces of sacred art were callously destroyed. This iconoclastic trend thus led to excesses of its own. Under the impact of modern individualism, Christians of recent centuries have fallen into an egocentric "me-and-Jesus" spirituality, neglecting horizontal relationships in the community. But in predominantly Catholic countries the sense of solidarity among all the redeemed has remained stronger, allowing the cult of the saints, purified of some medieval distortions, to remain vibrant.

In the decade after the Second Vatican Council (that is to say, from about 1965 to 1975) devotion to Mary and the saints suffered a marked decline, at least in Western Europe and North America. The reasons for this phenomenon are complex: an aspiration to renew the Church by returning to an early stage before these devotions had developed; a liturgical renewal that aimed to focus attention on God and on the mysteries of the life of Christ; an ecumenical spirit, seeking the greatest possible rapprochement with Protestantism; and perhaps a touch of secular agnosticism, which subjects all assertions about the "world beyond" to the corrosive acids of doubt. In great parts of the modern world, the predominant danger for Catholics is no longer that of superstitious excess but of skeptical minimalism. At least in the United States, religious individualism is a persistent temptation. This can be offset by cultivating a livelier sense of the communion of saints.

The Second Vatican Council, in its Constitution on the Church, set forth a strong but moderate position. It taught that the lives of those who have been transformed by grace into "particularly successful images of Christ" vividly manifest the presence and features of God. God speaks to us in them, and through them draws us powerfully to himself (LG 50). The Council pointed to Mary as the most excellent fruit of Christ's redemptive work, a faultless model of what the Church as a whole hopes to become (SC 103; cf. LG 65).

The saints form a great choir consisting of many voices — men and women, rich and poor, black and white, young and old; people of every race, nation, and language. All of them reflect the glory of God shining in the face of the incarnate Son. Like prisms in the sunlight, they refract the white light of Christ in multiple hues corresponding to their own particular gifts, abilities, and circumstances.

The variety of the saints is itself important in order that

the transformative power of the gospel may be shown forth in its plenitude. They provide examples to inspire and guide the faithful of every rank and condition. Among their number are martyrs, who joyfully laid down their lives for Christ, confessors who courageously proclaimed his name, and virgins who opted to follow him in consecrated celibacy. In the liturgical calendar of the saints we find popes, bishops, priests, religious, and, in small but increasing numbers, married men and women who were conscious of their duty to serve Christ under the conditions of secular life.

The saints, then, are vivid embodiments of the gospel. They exist primarily for God's sake, inasmuch as they glorify him by showing forth the power of his grace. They exist, secondly, for their own sake, since they attain blessedness by giving full scope to the working of the Holy Spirit within them. They exist, finally, for the sake of the Church and its members. They remind us of Christ, and thereby help us to trust in him. They sustain our hope by showing how much God's grace can accomplish in frail human nature. They keep us humble, by showing us how little we have done for Christ in comparison with them. By their boldness in following Christ they strengthen our resolve; they enlarge and correct our moral vision. They guide us by giving attractive examples suited to our needs and potentialities. They arouse in us the desire to do for our time and place what they did for theirs. And they also assist us by their prayers.

The Catholic Church believes and teaches that the saints are taken up into the life of glory, in which they are united forever with Christ their Lord. Christ, in heaven, is not idle, for according to Holy Scripture he is our advocate and intercessor. We have every reason, then, to believe that, as the Church teaches, the saints take part in this work of intercession. Since they are "in Christ," they do with and under Christ what they observe him doing. St. Thérèse of Lisieux, recently recognized as a Doctor of the Church, had a deep appreciation of the intercession of the saints. Just before her death she said: "I want to spend my heaven doing good on earth."

The manifold favors attributed to her intercession attest that she has been fulfilling this heavenly vocation.

Our communion with the saints involves not only their prayers for us, but also their presence in our prayer. Strictly speaking, all prayer is directed to God, but in praying to God we may invoke the intercession of the saints. We do not pray to the saints in the same way that we pray to God. We do not ask them to pardon our sins, to give us grace, or to bestow eternal life. All these gifts are proper to God alone. But with the assurance that they are still alive and conscious, and that they continue to seek what Christ seeks, we ask them to remember us whom they have left behind and to intercede for our needs and intentions with their divine Lord and ours. We look upon them as our older brothers and sisters, standing closer to the throne of grace now than when they were on earth.

Mary as Queen of the Saints

The Blessed Virgin Mary towers over all other members of the communion of saints. At her Annunciation she was hailed as "full of grace," highly favored by God. By responding to the angel's message with the words "let it be done to me according to your word," she manifested a humble obedience that the Fathers of the Church frequently contrast with the disobedience of Eve. When she came to visit her cousin Elizabeth before the birth of John the Baptist, Elizabeth was impelled to hail her as "blessed among women" because she had believed what was spoken to her, accepting it as a message from the Lord (Lk 1:42, 45). Responding to Elizabeth with the great hymn of the "Magnificat," Mary was inspired to foretell that all generations would call her blessed (Lk 1:46-55).

Mary's entire career was an extraordinary pilgrimage that carried her to the loftiest heights and the deepest abysses of faith. Together with moments of great joy and consolation, her life included many disappointments and puzzling reverses, to which Simeon alluded when he predicted that her soul would be pierced by a sword. The Gospels tell us that she had to flee with Joseph and the infant Jesus to the land of Egypt. When Jesus was still a boy of twelve, Mary and Joseph experienced the pain and anxiety of losing him in the Temple, a critical moment at which Jesus indicated to them his vocation to devote himself to the business of his heavenly Father.

Later Mary, so to speak, launched Jesus on his public life by providing the occasion for his first miracle at the wedding feast of Cana. She accompanied him in much of his ministry in Galilee and Judea, and at the end she and several of the holy women stood valiantly at the Cross after most of the male disciples had fled. From the Cross, John tells us, Jesus entrusted his Mother to the care of the Beloved Disciple, and in a special way placed that disciple under Mary's protection. In the days of prayer between the Ascension and Pentecost, Mary stayed with the disciples in the Upper Room in Jerusalem. She began at this point to appear in her role as Queen of the Apostles.

In the course of the centuries the Church has progressively come to realize that its own relationship to Jesus involves an intimate relationship with Mary as well. By her virginal motherhood Mary is the type and nucleus of the Church, which is Christ's immaculate and fruitful Bride. In her sinlessness and her glorious Assumption she is an unfailing source of hope for what the Church aspires to become. In heaven she continues in her role of petitioning her Son to show forth his power and his love, as she already did at Cana. She issues no commands, but always bids us to do whatever Jesus tells us (Jn 2:5). In her total subordination to Christ Mary epitomizes the mediation of the saints.

Long centuries were needed for the Church's teaching about Mary to mature. Only in the fifth century, at the Council of Ephesus (431), did the Church reach a consensus that Mary could properly be called not only Mother of Christ but also Mother of God, God-bearer. In 1854, after some seven hundred years of theological debate and clarification, the pope promulgated the dogma of the Immaculate Conception — that is to say, Mary's preservation from original sin by Christ's redemptive grace. The dogma of the Assumption, proclaimed in 1950, was less controversial. The belief that Mary, soon after her death, was glorified in body and soul had been widely accepted at least since the seventh century, and was uncontested in Roman Catholicism since the Middle Ages.

In 1964, at the end of the third session of the Second Vatican Council, Pope Paul VI bestowed on Mary the title "Mother of the Church." That title actually involved no new definition of faith, but a new authorization to think and speak of Mary as many were already doing. Her role as Mother of Christ in his physical body is extended to the Mystical Body, so that she is seen as Mother of Christians. All Christian believers, like the Beloved Disciple, are encouraged to seek her maternal intercession in time of need.

It is especially as virginal Mother that Mary typifies the Church. The Church, like Mary, has a bridal relationship to God. The more faithfully the Church preserves its purity and its trust in God's providential guidance, the more fruitful does the Church become. The active ministry of the hierarchy, which prolongs the ministry of Christ himself, is directed to the holiness of the Church's members, and is designed to serve it. Thus the "Marian" dimension of the Church is more fundamental and more precious than its apostolic dimension, typified by Peter.

The holiness of Mary does not belong to the same order as that of Jesus. He is the unique Mediator of all grace and forgiveness; she is the exemplary recipient. She is chosen by God from all eternity to be the bearer of the Son of God. Her dignity as Mother of the Lord is the ground of all her blessings. In terms of grace and glory she has nothing that she has not received from her Son. When we pray to Mary, we are simply asking her to pray for us and to obtain from her divine Son what he alone can give. She is not a goddess, but a suppliant, albeit a suppliant whose petitions, we are told, are never denied.

Devotion to the saints is a very personal thing, in which the Church encourages us to choose what we find most helpful for our own spiritual progress. The liturgy, as the public worship of the Church, is centered on God and on Christ as the Son of God, and refers to the saints only in a subordinate role. Liturgical prayer is rarely addressed to the saints, even verbally. It is normally addressed to the Father, through the Son, and in the Holy Spirit. The sacraments are acts of God and of Christ, not acts of the saints. But the liturgy provides a sanctoral cycle, which runs concurrently with the temporal cycle dealing with Christ and the Holy Spirit. The sanctoral cycle commemorates the saints, but only in a way subordinate to the mysteries of Christ, which are central in worship as well as in doctrine.

In seeking to relate themselves more closely to God and to Christ, Catholics find Mary and the saints to be helps, not hindrances. Believers are joyfully conscious of belonging to a world populated by holy friends whom they can admire, imitate, and rely upon for assistance. In their devotion to the saints they can err by excess or by falling short. The Church in its official actions has sometimes had to restrain superstitious excesses and at other times to encourage recourse to the example and assistance of the saints. A rightly ordered veneration of the saints cannot fail to be spiritually profitable.

Without the communion of saints the new world of faith would be incomplete. It might seem to be a mere wish, a human fantasy. But in union with the saints, the Church achieves its deepest purpose and realizes itself most perfectly. Our companionship with the saints unites us more closely to Christ, in whom every grace has its highest expression and its unfailing source.

Structures of the Church

In the last two chapters we have considered the Church primarily under the aspect of a Spirit-given communion of persons. But it is also an institution. Founded by Christ as a visible society and animated by the Holy Spirit, it is a sign and instrumental cause of the spiritual community — a communion of faith, hope, and love. Because of its vital relationship to Christ and the Holy Spirit, the Church, even in its visible aspect, is not a mere institution. It is, in the broad sense of the word, a "sacrament," that is to say, a visible, divinely established, efficacious sign of the invisible gifts of grace. The Church itself, as a kind of "general sacrament," is a sign charged with the reality of the grace that it communicates.

Church Structures

Jesus himself gave the Church its fundamental structures. He was aware that it could not survive as a worldwide community of faith and witness, enduring throughout all future history, unless it had firm structures — doctrinal, sacramental, and hierarchical. While laying down the basic patterns, Jesus allowed time for the Church to mature, perfecting its structures under the guidance of the Holy Spirit. In the Acts of the Apostles and the letters of Paul we can trace this process at work. The self-constitution of the Church continues through the next three centuries. By the middle of the fourth century, the Church may be said to have stabilized the main points of its heritage of doctrine, its sacramental forms of worship, and its papal-episcopal form of polity — though, of course, further refinements and adaptations will continue to be made as long as history lasts.

For a correct understanding of the structures of the Church, one must avoid the fallacy of primitivism. Christ laid the foundations but did not construct the entire edifice. He planted the seeds but left the full growth to later generations. Conscious that the apostles were not yet ready to receive all that he had to teach, he promised to send the Holy Spirit to supplement his teaching after the Ascension. In the New Testament we can glimpse the gradual emergence of certain structures that would not assume definitive form until some later time. We are the beneficiaries of these later developments. We cannot go back to the first century and begin again.

Jesus is often called a prophet, priest, and king. In his prophetic office he proclaimed a new message, epitomized in the parables and the Sermon on the Mount. As a "rabbi," he gave special instruction to the inner circle of his disciples. As priest, Jesus prayed, worshiped, and offered his own life to the Father to establish and seal the New Covenant. As king, he laid down rules of conduct for his disciples and all who would follow his new way of life. After his death he entered into his heavenly inheritance. From there he reigns over the whole world with power that will be made manifest when he appears once more in the glory of his Father.

The Teaching Office

The structures of the Church correspond to the three functions just mentioned. The Church is, in the first place, commissioned to preach and teach all that Christ revealed, including the completion of that revelation given in the death and resurrection of Jesus and in the sending of the Holy Spirit. The Church's teaching took time to crystallize. The development of the canon of Scripture played an important role in settling the Church's doctrine. In the first generations the Hebrew Scriptures were gradually supplemented with the four Gospels and the apostolic letters that formed the nucleus of what we call the "New Testament." For practical purposes, the canon may be regarded as fixed by about the end of the fourth century.

The faithful transmission of the Christian patrimony was assured not only by the norm of Scripture but also by baptismal confessions and creeds, which set the pattern for catechetical instruction. But the traditional creeds were not adequate to answer every question, especially those that arose in the light of Greek philosophy. We have already mentioned the contributions of the early ecumenical councils in settling debates about the Trinity and Christology, thereby safeguarding the unity of the Church and its fidelity to the revelation already given.

The unity and stability of faith required a voice that could authoritatively speak for the Church, an official teaching ministry in and for the Church. The bishops, together with their head, the bishop of Rome, constitute what is called, in contemporary usage, the "magisterium." As the official teachers of the Church, they have power to establish Catholic doctrine. Their teaching is not simply their own; it bears the authority of Christ and is the doctrine of the Church.

The words "He who hears you hears me" (Lk 10:16) apply in a special way to popes and bishops, because of their charisms of office. In language consecrated by ecumenical councils, the pope is held to be gifted with the "charism of truth and unfailing faith" (Vatican I); bishops are said to be endowed with the "sure charism of truth" (Vatican II, DV 8). More will be said about the exercise of the magisterium in Chapter 7.

The Priestly Office

The Church's priestly functions include liturgical prayer, the Holy Sacrifice of the Eucharist, and the sacraments. The Church's prayer is modeled on that of Christ the high priest, who offered prayers and supplications "in the days of his flesh" (Heb 5:7) and who continues to make intercession for those "who draw near to God through him" (Heb 7:25). The Gospels depict Jesus as frequently praying, and indeed spending the whole night in prayer to God (Lk 6:12). The Gospel of John recounts at length the high-priestly prayer in which Jesus at the Last Supper asked for the Father's grace and protection for the community of his disciples.

Not only did Jesus himself pray; he instructed his disciples to do likewise. The "Our Father," which he gave to them as their community prayer, remains to this day the most basic prayer of the Church and of individual Christians. Significantly, this prayer begins with three petitions for the glory of God and the realization of his Kingdom, and only then does it turn to the needs of the faithful. In these subsequent petitions the disciples are taught to ask to be delivered from sin and temptation but also to ask for their daily necessities.

The Church continually offers prayers to God, especially in the Eucharist and the Liturgy of the Hours. Like the apostles in Gethsemane, Christians are bidden to pray for themselves, lest they enter into temptation. They are also to pray for others, as Paul instructed Timothy: "I urge that supplications, prayers, intercessions, and thanksgivings be made for all men" (1 Tim 2:1).

Jesus repeatedly assures his disciples that what they ask in his name will be granted. In the new world of faith they are children of a loving and caring Father, who is able to provide for all their needs. But prayer is not magic. We always pray with the proviso that what we ask be truly for God's glory and for our good. Even Jesus, when beseeching his Father to be spared from his cruel death, saw fit to add: "Nevertheless, not as I will, but as thou wilt" (Mt 26:39). By prayer we obtain the strength to accept what God has in store for us. But prayer may be a source of other spiritual and material benefits. In his providence, God often reserves his choicest blessings to those who pray for them confidently and humbly, as beggars.

The sacraments are landmarks of the new world of faith. They are events of grace, in which Christ reactualizes the mystery of the Cross and Resurrection. Permanently present in the Church through his Holy Spirit, he acts in covenanted ways when the sacraments are rightly administered. Sacraments are therefore events of grace, personal encounters with the Lord. When received with the proper dispositions, the sacraments are transformative for those who participate in them.

The Church as a social community becomes publicly visible in its sacramental actions. In their ecclesial aspect, they are acts of the Church as such, in which the Church achieves maximum density and renews itself at the very sources of its being. The Christian community, celebrating the sacraments as public acts, solidifies the communion of its members in Christ the Lord.

Each sacrament conveys its own special grace. Three of the sacraments impart a special configuration to Christ the High Priest: baptism, confirmation, and holy orders. This configuration, technically known as a "sacramental character," is permanent, indelible, and unrepeatable. Whoever has validly received any one of these sacraments can never receive it again.

Baptism is the sacrament that brings us into the new world of faith. It is the basic sacrament of incorporation into the Body of Christ. Paul captures the meaning of this sacrament when he writes: "Do you not know that all of us who have been baptized into Christ were baptized into his death? We were buried therefore with him by baptism into death, so that as Christ was raised from the dead by the glory of the Father, we too might walk in newness of life" (Rom 6:3-4). So impressed is Paul by the newness that he writes: "If anyone is in Christ, he is a new creation; the old has passed away, behold, the new has come" (2 Cor 5:17).

Sometimes baptism is treated as if it were the celebration of the birth of a new child to a Christian couple. Even when administered to infants, it is much more than this. It is the sacrament of regeneration or rebirth. In the Holy Saturday proclamation the deacon sings: "Being born would have been no advantage for us unless we could have profited from being redeemed." For infants, baptism signifies, among other things, the incomparable blessing of being raised in the Church of Christ with access to all its treasures of truth and grace.

The use of water aptly symbolizes the cleansing from sin that baptism effects. Paul brings out this aspect when he reminds the Corinthians: "You were washed, you were sanctified, you were justified in the name of the Lord Jesus Christ and in the Spirit of our God" (1 Cor 6:11). Although the washing cancels out the guilt of original and personal sin, it does not remove the evil tendencies resulting from sin and the need to struggle for personal holiness.

Emphasizing the corporate significance of baptism, the First Letter of Peter dwells on the priestly dignity of all the baptized: "You are a chosen race, a royal priesthood, a holy nation, God's own people, that you may declare the wonderful deeds of him who called you out of darkness into his marvelous light. Once you were no people but now you are God's people" (1 Pt 2:9-10).

Baptism, as the fundamental sacrament of incorporation, is the gateway to the other sacraments. Inasmuch as it gives a share in Christ's priestly office, it equips its recipients to participate actively in Christian worship, for example, by joining in the offering of the Eucharist.

Confirmation, the second sacrament of initiation, was originally part of baptism, and consisted of the anointing of the baptized with chrism by the bishop. The separation of the two sacraments in the West came about for reasons that were primarily historical. In the Western churches confirmation was generally reserved to the bishop, and was delayed until such time as the bishop might be available to administer it. In the Eastern churches chrismation is usually performed by a priest, and is administered together with baptism.

The grace of confirmation is generally understood to consist in a deepening of the effects of baptism itself. It is a fuller incorporation into the body of Christ, a richer bestowal of the Holy Spirit. In the Western churches confirmation has been interpreted as qualifying its recipients to be witnesses to their faith, ready to confess it boldly in challenging situations. To be a Christian it is not enough to believe; one's belief should translate itself into word and action, according to the saying of Paul, "I believed, and so I spoke" (2 Cor 4:13, quoting Ps 116:10).

Since churches of the Latin rite usually delay confirmation until the candidate has arrived at the use of reason and can have an intention to receive the sacrament, it became possible in these churches to interpret confirmation as the sacrament of Christian maturity. On the ground that confirmed Christians have the mission to proclaim their faith publicly, the Church requires that the administration of this sacrament should be preceded by catechetical instruction in the faith. A child who had not reached the age of discretion and had not been instructed in the faith would not be ready to become a mature disciple and witness to Christ.

The third sacrament that imparts a permanent character is **ordination (holy orders)**. The character of ordination, like that of baptism or confirmation, configures its recipients to Christ the high priest. But it is a new configuration, qualitatively different from that of baptism or confirmation.

The fullness of the priesthood is given to bishops who, as previously stated, succeed to the apostles in the supreme direction of the universal Church. The head of the apostolic college is the bishop of Rome, the pope, who is the successor of Peter. The college cannot act as a whole without the participation and approval of the pope, since he is its head. If the pope dies while a council is in session, the council is automatically suspended until dissolved or reconvened by the next pope.

Canon law makes no provision for the highly unusual case of uncertainty about the identity of the legitimate pope. Such a case arose in 1414, when there were three claimants to the papal office. The emperor in concert with one of the claimants convened a general council, that of Constance. After one of the claimants resigned, the council deposed the other two and elected a new pope, Martin V. He and his successors retroactively approved some of the decrees passed during the period of uncertainty.

Presbyters (commonly called "priests" today, although the ancient Church more accurately referred to them as "priests of the second order") participate in the same sacrament that is administered in its fullness to bishops. Deacons are also sacramentally ordained, but their office is not priestly. They are usually assigned to ministries of the word and of charity. Bishops, priests, and deacons thus have three modes or degrees of the sacrament of holy orders.

These theological observations should make it clear that officeholders in the Church are not mere functionaries. They have received a sacrament that contains a promise of grace. Many of the Church's sacramental ministries (confirmation, the Eucharist, ordination, penance, and the anointing of the sick) require celebrants who are in priestly or episcopal orders.

The priest is consecrated in such a way that he represents Christ to the community. When he teaches, governs, or administers the sacraments, he acts by the authority of Christ. The priest can also act in the name of the Church, when he prays and offers the eucharistic sacrifice to God for the community of the faithful.

From the earliest days, the Church has selected only men for the episcopal and presbyteral offices. Although the question of a female priesthood has arisen many times in the course of the centuries, the bishops and theologians have been virtually unanimous in responding that only men could be ordained. Following the Fathers of the first few centuries, medieval theologians such as Thomas Aquinas, Bonaventure, and Duns Scotus all sought to give theological explanations for this immemorial practice. Many scholars contend that the male sex alone is fitting, since the priest represents Christ precisely in his capacity as Bridegroom of the Church, who offers the sacrifice by which he sanctifies his beloved bride, in order to make her holy and without blemish (cf. Eph 5:25-27). In 1994 Pope John Paul II taught that the testimony of Scripture, confirmed by the constant and universal teaching of the magisterium, excludes the possibility of women priests in the Catholic Church.

The fourth sacrament, that of **marriage (matrimony)**, like other sacraments, needs to be understood with reference to Christ and the Church. Even couples who get married in the Church often fail to realize the important place of this sacrament in the new world of faith. It is much more than a blessing conferred by the Church on a purely human union. As Paul taught, Christian marriage is a "great mystery" or sacrament; it is a living image of the indissoluble union and mutual self-giving of Christ and the Church (cf. Eph 5:32-33). Sexual love is purified and elevated to a higher level in Christ and the Church. The partners freely make a permanent, unreserved, and exclusive gift of themselves to each other — a gift that will often be blessed by fruitfulness in the begetting of children. A union that is intended to be temporary, conditional, or nonexclusive does not fulfill the Christian concept of marriage.

God calls man and woman in marriage to "be fruitful and multiply, and fill the earth and subdue it" (Gen 1:28). By their free cooperation in transmitting the gift of human life parents are privileged to share in the creative power of God himself. Marriage is intended for the procreation and raising of children. It is debased if the partners use one another simply as means of pleasure and self-satisfaction. When there are serious reasons for limiting the number of children, family planning that makes use of the natural rhythms of fertility may be justified.

Sexual activity, according to Catholic teaching, is forbidden except within marriage, where it is allowed only in acts that are open to procreation. Contraception, since it violates the integrity of the conjugal act, is prohibited. Some so-called contraceptives are in fact abortifacients, since they kill the unborn child in the very early stages of its development. Contraception and abortion, though they differ in kind and in gravity, stem from the same hedonistic attitude: they manifest a similar refusal to accept responsibility in matters of sexuality. Persons who practice contraception are tempted to have recourse to abortion when contraception fails. More will be said about abortion below, in Chapter 10.

The Church understands that the call to chastity, both for the married and for the unmarried, is a difficult one, calling for struggle and self-discipline, especially on the part of young people. Men and women of good character will often sin against chastity, as against other virtues. When this happens, they are, or should be, conscious of deserving punishment. The wonderful thing about the new world of faith is that God, in place of punishment, offers forgiveness to those who turn to him in repentance. Because Christ in his suffering and death paid a superabundant price for all the sins of the world, God is always prepared to offer forgiveness.

Christ instituted a special sacrament, commonly known as that of **penance**, or **reconciliation**, in which those who had sinned might receive assurance of forgiveness and be restored to full communion with the Church. Forgiveness necessarily has an ecclesial dimension, because sin is an offense against the Church as well as against God. It impairs the communion of saints; it diminishes the holiness of the Church and the credibility of its witness. Because the Church is inalienably holy in its essence, every sin estranges the sinner in some measure from the Church.

Presupposing an examination of conscience, this sacrament includes four elements. It begins with contrition, that is to say, sincere sorrow accompanied by an intention to avoid sin in the future. Then follows confession, in which the penitent submits his or her sins to the tribunal of God's mercy and healing. The priest, as the minister of Christ and of the Church, then grants absolution. Finally, the penitent performs some work of satisfaction. This may involve reparation for the harm done to other people or may take the form of some pious work, such as prayer, fasting, or almsgiving, as a token of the renunciation of sin and of commitment to life in union with Christ.

Christ in his earthly ministry showed particular compassion on the sick and infirm. When he sent out his apostles, he instructed them to anoint the sick with oil and heal them (Mk 6:13). In the early Church, presbyters were instructed to anoint the sick with oil in the name of the Lord (Jas 5:14).

The sacramental **anointing of the sick**, based on these biblical foundations, is intended for physical healing, if God so wills, but in any case for strengthening the sick to bear their suffering with hope and patience. It configures the suffering of the sick to the redemptive Passion of our Lord, so that the anointed person may find, as did Paul, that God's power is made perfect in human weakness (2 Cor 12:9) and that it is possible through suffering to complete in one's flesh "what is lacking in Christ's afflictions for the sake of his body, that is, the church" (Col 1:24).

When administered to the dying, as is sometimes the case, the anointing of the sick should be followed by Holy Communion as the final preparation for entry into the heavenly homeland.

I have reserved to the last the sacrament of the **Eucharist**, although it is, after baptism and confirmation, one of the three sacraments of Christian initiation. Thomas Aquinas wrote that "the Eucharist is the consummation of the spiritual life and the destination of all the sacraments, which either prepare us to receive the Eucharist or to consecrate it" (*Summa theologiae,* III, qu. 73, art. 3).

Christ is present in every sacrament, at least in a dynamic manner, as acting through and in the rite. But in the

Eucharist he makes himself present substantially, in the sense that the bread and wine become, in their inmost reality perceptible only to faith, his very self. The Holy Spirit is active in bringing about the sacramental sacrifice and the Real Presence.

The Eucharist is the sacrament of the New Covenant par excellence, since Christ sealed God's covenant with the Church, the new Israel, by the shedding of his blood. Speaking of the bread as "my body which is for you" and of the chalice as "the new covenant in my blood" (1 Cor 11:24-25 and parallels), Jesus indicated that the Eucharist was a memorial in which he would perpetuate his presence precisely as covenant-partner, in his nuptial relationship with the Church.

In its ecclesial aspect the Eucharist is a public action in which the Church realizes itself as community. The bishop or celebrating priest, standing at the altar, surrounded by other members of the clergy, joins with the entire congregation in offering the holy sacrifice. The sacrifice is actually brought about by the words of consecration, pronounced by a validly ordained priest. As the "sacrament of ecclesiastical unity" the Eucharist is celebrated in union with the universal Church. One of its prime effects is to solidify the union of minds and hearts of those who receive.

By means of the Eucharist, Christ enables the Church to offer his own sacrifice to God in an "unbloody" manner. The congregation should take the occasion to offer themselves and their sufferings in union with the host on the altar. The Eucharist recalls the action of Jesus at the Last Supper as well as at Calvary; it also looks forward to the "supper of the Lamb" that will be celebrated unceasingly in heaven.

We should approach the sacrament with lively sentiments of faith, reverence, and gratitude, recognizing our unworthiness and repenting of our sins. We shall profit to the extent that we are rightly disposed, hungering for the Christ who deigns to make himself our food and to enter into a union with us so close that it may be called physical. It is a privileged moment for prayer and adoration. The abiding Real Presence of Christ in the tabernacle after the conclusion of the Mass enables the faithful to visit the reserved Sacrament and enter into prayerful conversation with the Lord as their divine companion.

To live in the new world of faith is to inhabit the territory defined by the seven sacraments. They are the points at which Christ is most palpably present and active in his Church. They bring us out of our petty and selfish concerns, so that we live no longer to ourselves but to Christ in union with the whole company of the redeemed. It is especially through the sacraments, one may say, that the Church becomes the communion of the saints.

The Ruling Office

To conclude this chapter, something should be said about the Church's structures of government, which correspond to some extent with the ruling office of Christ. Jesus saw the necessity of an authority that would hold his followers together in a single fellowship, faithful to the mission to which he had assigned them. He conferred on the Twelve and their successors authority to "bind" and "loose" (Mt 18:18), and in a special way he committed to Peter the power of the keys (Mt 16:19). He taught that those who would not listen to the Church should be treated as if they did not belong to the company of believers (Mt 18:17).

From the day of Pentecost the Church was governed by the apostles and persons whom they brought into association with themselves. The Twelve formed a stable group, a "college," with Peter at their head. In every listing of the apostles in the New Testament, Peter's name comes first, for he was the one chosen by Jesus to be the "rock" on which the Church was founded (Mt 16:18). He alone received the mission to "strengthen [his] brethren" so that their faith would not fail (Lk 22:32), and the charge of feeding the whole flock of Christ (Jn 21:15-17).

Since Christ had promised to be with the apostolic leadership until the end of the world, it was important to provide replacements for those who fell away, like Judas, or who died, as they all eventually did. Gradually the college of bishops, with the pope as its head, came to be recognized as succeeding to, or rather perpetuating, the apostolic office. The ecumenical councils that began to meet periodically after the acceptance of Christianity in the Roman Empire were made up of bishops as voting members. The bishop of Rome, as the primate of the universal Church, usually sent a delegate to represent him, and reserved the power to approve or disapprove the decrees personally. In a sense, therefore, his was the decisive voice even at ecumenical councils he did not attend.

Although the Church borrowed certain titles and practices from Judaism and from Greco-Roman political societies, its style of government — under a sacramentally ordained, self-perpetuating hierarchy — was something new in the world. The ecclesiastical hierarchy, as a college with and under the successor of Peter, cannot be equated with the institutions of rabbinic Judaism, and still less with secular judicial systems or secular states, whether monarchies, oligarchies, or democracies. Although Church government displays analogies with all of these styles of polity, it has its own singular features.

Among people not familiar with theology there is a tendency to think of authority in the Church as though it were the equivalent of political sovereignty. In the Church, however, God alone is sovereign. Christ himself, in his earthly career, took on the form of a servant, and proposed his own humble service as a model for his apostles. He insisted that the apostles were not to be called lords or masters; they were subject to his authority and were servants of the community. There was to be no contention among them for positions of power and honor.

The term "jurisdiction" is often used to describe the power of popes and bishops to make binding laws and issue strict commands. But jurisdiction in the Church differs from anything known to secular society. It is strictly circumscribed by its purpose, which is to direct souls into the ways of Christ. All authority in the Church is pastoral. Following the example and precepts of the Good Shepherd, pastors are to refrain from lording it over those committed to their care and are to be examples of selfless devotion.

Occasionally, of course, Church authorities have to use severity to protect the faithful against individuals or groups who would disrupt the community, harm its members, or impede its mission. For this reason there are canonical penalties such as deposition from office, removal of ecclesiastical faculties, suspension, interdict, and excommunication. But these penalties are administered in a paternal way, always with concern for the personal dignity and spiritual good of the person penalized. Church authorities impose penalties only with reluctance, preferring to use what Pope John XXIII, in his opening speech at Vatican II, called "the medicine of mercy." In the 1983 revision of the Code of Canon Law, efforts were made to eliminate punishments that might seem arbitrary, harsh, or degrading.

In a Church of sinners, those holding pastoral office do not always live up to the standards proposed for them. Laws and administrative procedures are periodically revised so as to prevent abuses of power. But these efforts will never be completely successful so long as the Church is immersed in the ambiguities of history. Sometimes it happens that individuals suffer unjustly at the hands of other Christians, and even at the hands of official leaders. They may be able to find remedies through recourse to higher authorities, but at times they may be called by the Lord to suffer in patience, thus imitating him in his Passion. One of the consolations of the gospel is its assurance that undeserved suffering can be a path to holiness.

Even though the structures can be misused, and occasionally are, that possibility does not cancel out their immense value in keeping the flock of Christ in the path of truth and in a vibrant community of faith and love. The prophetic, priestly, and ruling offices of the Church, together with the deposit of faith and sacraments, have never ceased to function as channels of divine grace. Without them the world of faith would lose its contours and fade into the shadows.

Handing Down the Faith

As the bearer of the new world of faith, the Church perpetually lives off its own origins, which have been given once and for all in Christ and the apostles. In several passages the New Testament speaks of faith as a trust or "deposit" to be faithfully preserved and handed on (1 Tim 6:20; 2 Tim 1:14). This deposit of faith is enshrined in Holy Scripture and perpetuated by living tradition. Taken together, Scripture and tradition are the principal means by which the faith is transmitted from generation to generation. But some explanation is necessary to indicate the nature and authority of each of these channels.

Scripture

Holy Scripture is not simply a product of the Church. It is produced within the community of faith by the power of God, and is to be treasured as his gift. God in his gracious providence controlled the composition of the biblical books so that they would contain a reliable record of his progressive revelation to his chosen people. They also attest to that people's faith as it developed over the centuries, from the time of the patriarchs to that of the apostles.

Not everything, of course, was present from the beginning. In the early strata of the Old Testament we are allowed to glimpse the difficult entry of God's revealed word into a primitive culture that was in many respects barbaric. The history is recounted realistically, so that we see the vices and defects of the people as well as their virtues and merits. From a Christian point of view the remarkable thing is the way in which the persons, events, things, and sayings of the Old Testament point forward in type and prophecy to their fulfillment in the New. St. Paul felt entitled to say that incidents in the Old Testament were recounted for the instruction of Christians as the elect people of the final age (1 Cor 10:11). The prophetic writings contained a mystery that was disclosed only when Christ appeared (Rom 16:25-27).

Again in the New Testament, revelation is presented dynamically in the process of its communication to people who were not entirely prepared for it. At first, even the apostles had difficulty comprehending the real message of Jesus, but its meaning gradually became clearer to them after the Resurrection, thanks to the assistance of the Holy Spirit. Very often the later books of the New Testament exhibit a clearer grasp of God's word than the books written closest to the events.

The New Testament, although inspired by the Holy Spirit, is at the same time a very human document. It manifests the human characteristics, even the failings, of the early Christians — their anger and their disappointments, as well as the tensions in the Church, including the apostasy of some believers. In this way the New Testament prepares us to cope with the mixture of faith and infidelity, holiness and sin, that characterizes the community of Christ's disciples in every age.

The inspiration of the Bible does not mean that it was

simply dictated from heaven. The authors, scribes, and editors of the biblical books had as much to do with their texts as do the composers of uninspired books. The difference is that they were providentially chosen and directed, so that they wrote what God wanted preserved for the guidance of the Church of later generations.

For the most part the Bible consists of stories from which the readers can draw their own conclusions. Sometimes the writers are simply making conjectures or expressing feelings without apparently intending to impose on their readers any obligation to share these views or sentiments. And at other times they are insistently declaring the contents of divine revelation, asking that their words be accepted as the word of God.

The Bible is often said to be free from error. This is true in the sense that everything in it is of value for our spiritual benefit, or, as Paul writes to Timothy, "profitable for teaching, for reproof, for correction, and for training in righteousness, that the man of God may be complete, equipped for every good work" (2 Tim 3:16-17). We are not entitled to expunge anything from the Bible or to alter it to fit our tastes. Properly used, everything in it can be helpful for Christian faith, morality, and worship. We must also acknowledge that what the Scriptures as a whole formally teach is the teaching of God himself. The Church therefore relies heavily on Scripture in drawing up its creeds and dogmas. It is careful never to contradict the formal teaching of Scripture and it regularly seeks to find a biblical basis for its teaching.

The value of the Bible does not consist simply in the bare fact of inspiration, which affects all the books in all their parts. That value is enhanced by the personal gifts of the prophets, psalmists, apostles, and other outstanding individuals whose work has found its way into many portions of the text. These leaders were moved by the Spirit to speak with exceptional power and insight about the ways of God with his people. The stories and images of Holy Scripture continue to engage the attention, fire the imagination, and inspire the devotion of readers many centuries later. In a memorable text, the Constitution on Divine Revelation stated:

> In the sacred books, the Father who is in heaven meets his children with great love and speaks with them; and the force and power in the word of God is so great that it remains the support and energy of the Church, the strength of faith for her children, the food of the soul, the pure and perennial source of spiritual life.
>
> — DV 21

The Christian Church in its early years simply took over the Hebrew Bible. Most Christians used that Bible in existing Greek versions that did not exactly correspond to the versions being used in Judea. The Christian Church felt free to choose from among the Jewish Scriptures those that it regarded as consonant with Christian doctrine and as pointing forward to the final revelation of God in Jesus Christ. On the whole these were the books that Jesus and the apostles read and cited as Scripture. Most of them were eventually included in the Jewish canon, which had not yet been settled in the time of Jesus.

When Christians began to deliberate about the list of books they were to use as Holy Scripture, they already had their faith, which they had received through the apostles and the evangelists, catechists, and presbyters whom the apostles enlisted as their delegates or assistants. Toward the end of the first century the Christians began to collect writings of the foundational period that gave a reliable and inspiring record of the apostolic Church and its teaching. To begin with, the various local churches made their own collections, but, bound together by a network of communion, they gradually came to recognize and accept one another's lists of Scripture. In this way the universal Church developed a biblical canon consisting of two Testaments — an Old and a New. Following a series of local councils going back as far as the fourth century, the Council of Trent in the sixteenth century pronounced definitively on the list of canonical books.

The Bible is not intended to be a complete or systematic inventory of Christian doctrine, though, of course, it attests to the essentials of Jewish and Christian faith. In using it, the Christians saw it as confirming, enriching, and illustrating the faith that was already theirs, thanks to the transmission of the apostolic preaching. The New Testament was a privileged and, indeed, inspired sedimentation or deposit of the faith of the early Church. The Church read Holy Scripture not in isolation but in the context of its own faith. From their living faith, sustained by the Holy Spirit, Christians derived their capacity to recognize the inspired Scriptures and interpret them faithfully.

Disputes, of course, arose from time to time about what the Bible really taught. Different texts seemed to point in different directions. For example, was Jesus equal in dignity to the Father or inferior to the Father? Was he the uncreated Son or a creature? Was the Holy Spirit God or a created energy emanating from God? Did Mary remain a virgin throughout life or did she have other children, brothers and sisters of Jesus? Were infants conceived and born in a state of sin? Questions such as these, unsettled in the early Church, were gradually resolved by councils after lengthy discussion.

Tradition

Since Scripture by itself did not seem to give clear answers to these questions, the Church did not rely on Scripture alone as its source. It drew heavily on traditions that were thought to have come down from apostolic times. Apostolic tradition did not function as a totally independent source, but it often tipped the balance in cases where the interpretation of Scripture was disputed.

The concept of tradition has itself evolved over the centuries. Initially, the term was generally used in the plural; it referred to specific apostolic teachings, especially those not contained in Holy Scripture. But in contemporary usage the term is generally used in the singular with a capital T, to designate the corporate life and usages of the Church as the framework within which the written documents of faith are interpreted. Tradition is known not so much by looking at it as by dwelling in it as a kind of "spiritual house" in which one lives. Sustained in the Church by the Holy Spirit, Tradition is a dynamic, growing reality.

According to the Second Vatican Council, Tradition develops in the Church with the help of the Holy Spirit (DV 8). By their prayerful study of Scripture and their participation in the life and worship of the Church, the faithful gain deeper insights into the meaning of God's word. But it is also possible for particular traditions — those that are ephemeral or merely local — to be deficient and in need of correction in the light of the gospel.

Among the sources of Christian doctrine we must reckon, in close relationship with Scripture and Tradition, the liturgy. The public prayer of the Church is a fruitful source for explicit teaching. The Church has often defended and developed its doctrine by pointing out what is implied in the approved modes of worship. Several cases may be given to illustrate this process.

In its struggle against the Arians, who held that the Father alone was God, early champions of the Trinity pointed out that Christians were always baptized in the name of the Father, the Son, and the Holy Spirit. Catholic theologians argued that because candidates for baptism professed without distinction their faith in the Father, the Son, and the Holy Spirit, in whose "name" they were about to be baptized, it followed that all three persons were truly and equally divine.

In the debates about original sin, orthodox bishops such as Augustine argued that because infants were baptized "for the remission of sins," they were evidently born under the power of sin. In further arguments with the Pelagians about whether grace was necessary for conversion to the faith, Augustine and his party contended that the affirmative answer was proved from the practice of the Church in praying for the conversion of unbelievers, as it did in the Good Friday intercessions, following the precept of Paul in 1 Timothy 2:1-4. This appeal to liturgy as a source for doctrine has continued down through the centuries.

Still another important source for the vindication and development of doctrine is the "sense of the faithful" or the "consensus of the faithful." The argument is drawn up on the principle that the Holy Spirit, dwelling in the Church, moves the members to assent to matters of faith with ease and joy. They have in their hearts a kind of instinct prompting them to believe what truly belongs to the faith and inclining them to reject as a foreign substance whatever clashes with that faith.

Abraham Lincoln once declared that you can fool some of the people all of the time, and all of the people some of the time, but you cannot fool all of the people all of the time. Something analogous holds for the Church. Although individual believers can easily be misled by particular circumstances, and the whole body may be thrown off course for a short while, the entire body of the faithful cannot be deceived about the content of the faith over a long period of time. In the fifth century, Vincent of Lerins formulated the dictum that Christians were obliged to accept what has been believed in the Church "everywhere, always, and by all."

In 1859 John Henry Newman wrote a famous article "On Consulting the Faithful in Matters of Doctrine." He contended that such consultation was particularly useful for doctrines with devotional implications, such as beliefs concerning the Blessed Virgin and the saints. As an example he cited the eagerness with which devout Christians anticipated the recognition of Mary as Mother of God by the Council of Ephesus in 431, and their joy when they heard that the dogma had been proclaimed.

Another of Newman's examples is the dogma of the Immaculate Conception. It was deeply inscribed in the hearts of the faithful before it was accepted by the magisterium as a revealed truth. Before defining it, Pope Pius IX wrote to all the bishops of the world asking whether they and the faithful of their dioceses believed that the doctrine was true and that it ought to be defined as a matter of faith. He went ahead after receiving an overwhelmingly positive response.

The application of the "sense of the faithful" is not free from difficulty. We have to consider, in the first place, who count as the faithful — a term that should be understood as referring to Christians who let their views be formed by the gospel and the teaching of the Church. Not everything that the faithful believe is the fruit of their faith. Influenced by the general culture, they tend to accept as true what they imbibe from popular presentations of science and history, at their current state of development. They commonly subscribe to the maxims of the world, which are often false and deceptive. To be theologically significant, the views would have to be inspired by faith. There is no "sense of the faithful" that is not, more fundamentally, a "sense of the faith" — a sense of what faith itself inclines one to believe.

Secondly, the sense of the faithful is essentially Church-related. As a "sense of the faith," it coincides with the spontaneous convictions of orthodox believers. In its full scope it implies agreement between those holding pastoral office and other believers, religious and lay. It is not a matter of the majority of laypeople outvoting the pope and the bishops. Unless the clergy as well as the laity freely accept the teaching, it cannot be a matter of consensus.

Normally, the sense of the faithful develops through harmonious interaction between the hierarchy and the rest of the faithful. The hierarchy teaches something, for example, the divinity of Christ or the maternity of Mary. Then the faithful respond by accepting and perhaps enriching or nuancing the teaching. When, for instance, they are taught that Christ is God and that Mary is Christ's mother, they conclude that Mary is the Mother of God. As a result of the feedback, the magisterium takes the further step of conferring a new title upon Mary and condemning the view that Mary was the mother only of Christ's humanity.

Thirdly, the consent of the faithful may be a long time in the making. Often enough, doctrines of the faith begin as minority opinions and only gradually win general consent. It would be wrong to conclude that because a doctrine has not won general consent in the Church, it is probably false. The resistance may come not from the "instinct of faith" but from people's selfish desires or their proneness to follow contemporary secular opinion.

Magisterium

An indispensable role in the transmission and development of doctrine is played by the hierarchical magisterium. Without it the Church would have no way of certifying its corporate faith. To some extent, the faith is expressed in Holy Scripture, but the magisterium was needed to identify the Scriptures and attest to their inspiration. The authoritative interpretation of Scripture is the prerogative of the magisterium. In formulating Catholic doctrine the magisterium relies not on Scripture alone but also on tradition, on approved liturgies, and on the sense of the faithful. To distinguish between valid traditions and tainted or distorted traditions is preeminently the task of the magisterium.

Although the hierarchical magisterium enjoys graces of office that assist it in the preservation of the deposit of faith, it does not have a magical access to truth. The Holy Spirit impels the pastors to use means suitable for the particular case. Some things are evidently clear from Scripture itself; others, from long-standing and unanimous tradition; still others are evident from right reason. The bishops consult among themselves, and the pope consults formally and informally with bishops. Both the pope and bishops consult with Scripture scholars and theologians and, when appropriate, sound out the views of the laity. But the final authority to pronounce on doctrinal matters rests with the ecclesiastical magisterium.

It is almost self-evident that God, if he intended to reveal any definite doctrinal truths for the benefit of humankind, would provide a reliable means for the preservation and transmission of those truths throughout the centuries. This he did, Catholics believe, by giving the apostles and their successors authority to teach in his name and by promising to be with them forever. As noted in Chapter 6, the hierarchical teachers do not teach simply in their own name or as ecclesiastical bureaucrats. Inducted into office by sacramental ordination, and endowed with a "sure charism of truth," they teach by the authority of Christ himself.

Thanks to their charisms of office, the pope and the whole body of bishops are able, under certain circumstances, to speak with infallibility. We should not allow ourselves to be frightened by the heated controversies surrounding this term. It is simply another way of saying that the Holy Spirit will preserve the Church against using its full authority to require its members to assent to what is false. If this could happen, the truth of revelation would not be preserved in recognizable form.

The magisterium rarely invokes its power to teach infallibly, and then only after long and careful consultation. The vast majority of Church teaching is proposed without any claim to infallibility, but it is difficult to find instances of error in the noninfallible teaching of popes and councils. Doctrine does, of course, develop, but not by way of reversal. As a result of more careful reflection and discussion, teachings originally proposed in a vague or imprecise manner come to be more fully understood, more profoundly stated, more carefully nuanced, and applied to new conditions. The experience of the Church over the centuries contributes significantly to its capacity to find new implications in the revelation committed to it. Biblical exegetes and theologians normally assist the hierarchical magisterium by their technical skills. They are often called upon to investigate the biblical and historical foundations or to find apt language for expressing the mind of the Church. After a doctrine is promulgated, they have an important role in teaching, explaining, and defending it. The normal relationship between theologians and the magisterium is one of cooperation.

Occasionally it happens that certain theologians find it difficult to assent to a given teaching of the magisterium. In such cases they should not leap to the conclusion that the magisterium has erred. The charism of judging the truth of doctrine is given primarily to the pope and the bishops, not to theologians. Theologians, like other members of the faithful, should try to see the truth or credibility of the official teaching. If they have difficulties, they may express them to colleagues and to the hierarchical teachers. In this way they may find ways of overcoming their objections, or they may help the magisterium to find a more convincing and accurate way of expressing its position. Over the centuries, the magisterium has been able to profit from the feedback that comes, so to speak, from the pews.

What is unhelpful is for theologians to engage in noisy protests and try to recruit adherents for their dissenting positions. It is especially harmful when they try to bring pressure on the magisterium by organizing rallies, calling press conferences, or placing paid advertisements in newspapers. The Church, unlike political society, is a community of faith held together by the shared beliefs and mutual love of its members. When the Church becomes a battlefield between opposed groups, sowing discord and antipathy, it becomes less appealing to its own members and less attractive to others whom it is commissioned to evangelize.

As believers, we have every reason to be grateful to the magisterium for having preserved the apostolic deposit of faith from erosion or corruption from generation to generation. The magisterium may not always say exactly what we think we would say if we were in a position to determine the official teaching. But it is a good thing that the magisterium does not allow itself to be swayed by every shifting current of public opinion. We want an authority that transmits a wisdom superior to our own. A Church that responded to our every wish would not be worth having. It would not be able to teach us, to change us, and to offer us salvation. A teaching office that mirrored public opinion in the world would be equally useless. It would have no message for the world. The message preached by the Church must always be something challenging and original, something that speaks to its hearers about the new world of faith. Without the resources of Scripture, Tradition, and the magisterium, the People of God would not long be able to resist the pressure to fall back into the old world from which Christ came to rescue them.

By faithfully adhering to what was given once for all in Christ, the Church retains its vitality and its capacity to judge the signs of the times in the light of the new and eternal gospel. The Word of God, as perpetuated in the Church, never ceases to anticipate and illumine the shape of things to come. By bestowing the Holy Spirit, Christ makes the Church equal to the challenges of every age and points the way into the eternal future, where he reigns at the right hand of the Father.

8 The Mission to Evangelize

Conscious of the commission of Christ to bring the gospel to all nations (Mt 28:19; Lk 24:47), to the whole creation (Mk 16:15), to the end of the earth (Acts 1:8), Christians down through the centuries have made heroic efforts to spread the word of God. They have undertaken long, arduous, and perilous journeys and in many cases suffered shipwreck, imprisonment, exile, torture, and martyrdom as the price of their fearless proclamation. Their efforts have been blessed in such a way that Christianity became, and remains to our own day, the largest of world religions. All of us who are believers today have to thank the brave and generous missionaries who brought the faith to our ancestors and our part of the world.

In recent years the opportunities for evangelization have vastly increased. Messages travel with the speed of light. Jet planes have made transportation swift, safe, and comfortable. Translation is far easier today than in an age when there were no dictionaries and few, if any, interpreters. But many Christians no longer seem to see the urgency to evangelize. Even in their own homes they make little effort to pass on the faith to their children. In traditionally Christian countries, many young people are no longer brought up in the faith. If the Christian portion of the world is not to shrivel, the sources of current doubt about the value of this holy apostolate must be openly confronted.

Obstacles to Evangelization

Among the obstacles to evangelization we must certainly reckon the three mentioned at the beginning of Chapter 1: historical consciousness, pluralism, and the free market of ideas. We shall do well to examine these phenomena more closely.

The spread of historical consciousness has made us acutely sensitive to the mutability of all things human. It has led many to ask whether the faith of our forebears is still valid. Do not all religions, like cultures and philosophical systems, have their day? Religions rise, they prosper, and at length they die. Is not Christianity destined to be cast someday into the ash heap of dead religions? Why should we spend our energies promoting a faith that is moribund? Let us look to the future, they say, not cling blindly to the past.

If Christianity were a merely human phenomenon, the objection would be plausible, though it could be argued that even a humanly concocted religion might enshrine permanently valid insights. However that may be, great religions such as Hinduism, Buddhism, and Islam, as well as Christianity, have a way of surviving over the millennia with little or no loss of impact. Authentic religion is based not on transitory circumstances but on constants of the human situation and on God's unfailing goodness. Christianity, as a specially revealed religion, cannot be treated as though it were a purely human concoction. God, the Lord of history, is capable of revealing something enduringly true and of preserving that truth throughout the centuries. Christ, as the incarnation of the eternal Son, can give a message that meets the longing of the human mind for imperishable truth. Historicism unwarrantably assumes that all faith is tied to its date of origin.

Pluralism grows out of the same general mentality as historicism. It compounds the problem by advocating simultaneous as well as successive relativism. Christianity, according to pluralists, perceives the divine from one particular angle, but in no way comprehends it. Other religions are thought to be necessary for supplementing what is lacking in Christianity. If all people became Christians, we are told, Christianity itself would be impoverished, since it would lack partners from whom to learn. Religious dialogue, in this theory, ought to replace missionary proclamation.

Tempting though this position is, it cannot be accepted without qualification. Christianity stands or falls with the claim that it is the definitive revelation of God and that its beliefs are true for people of every race and nation. If it is true for you and me that God is three-personed and that Jesus Christ, God's only Son, has become incarnate, lived, and died for the redemption of the human race, these beliefs are true for everyone and ought to be shared as widely as possible. Anyone who fails to acknowledge these revealed truths is, to that extent, not in the truth.

Christian faith in no way requires us to deny the existence of valid elements in other religions. People of every culture, sincerely seeking communion with the divine, may be expected to arrive at some measure of truth. God himself, very likely, comes to the aid of honest seekers, giving them intimations of the mysteries of grace. Christianity, at least in its Catholic form, has normally been solicitous not to reject anything good and true in other faiths. The Second Vatican Council, following some of the early Church Fathers, spoke of "rays of divine truth" shed by the Light of the World and "seeds of the Word" strewn by the divine Sower among the customs and religions of the world. These gifts should be seen not as substitutes but rather as preparations for the gospel, in the sense that they prepare people to receive the Good News of Jesus Christ.

What cannot be maintained is that contradictories are simultaneously true. Where two religions teach contradictorily opposed doctrines, one or the other, if not both, must be false. For this reason religious pluralism is problematical. The oppositions must be frankly faced and, so far as possible, overcome by dialogue. In interreligious dialogue Christians, like others, must strive to give a reason for the faith that is in them. Dialogue, therefore, does not take the place of proclamation. It involves proclamation as an inner moment of itself.

There is a grain of truth in the objection that no one religion offers the totality of truth concerning God. Although we cannot fathom the reasons why God in his providence has allowed so many religions to exist, one reason may be the value of other religions for enriching Christianity itself. By encountering them the Church may discover truths that have not yet been explicitly stated by Christians, and perhaps truths that the Church has not yet been prepared to accept. But a Christianity that has been educated through dialogue, as ancient Christianity was by Hellenistic philosophies, may be prudently receptive to insights from other faiths. Paul, looking forward to the eventual conversion of the Jews, writes: "If their failure means riches for the Gentiles, how much more will their full inclusion mean!" (Rom 11:12). Christianity grows stronger by borrowing what is sound from other religions, but weakens itself whenever it allows its members to accept elements that cannot be harmoniously integrated into Christian faith. Careful discernment is needed to exclude superstition and false syncretism.

The free-market conception of religion, which constitutes our third major objection, rests on the supposition that religion is a commodity to be advertised and sold, and that people, as religious consumers, are entitled to choose a religion according to their tastes. This view involves a cynical disregard for truth and a fallacious theory of freedom. Believers do not have a right to market anything that can be sold, packaging it in alluring ways. They must declare the whole counsel of God, in season and out of season. Nor do "consumers" in the religious market have the right to choose any church or belief system that makes them feel better. They have a duty to submit to that which they can recognize as true and good. Religious truth, to be sure, ought not to be forced on anyone, but it should be offered in such a way that people can recognize its exigent claims. The freedom of individuals is not diminished but rather increased when they are informed of the importance of accepting a definite revealed religion. Christian proclamation opens up the possibility for people to enter the new world of faith, which would otherwise be closed to them.

Behind many of the contemporary hesitations about evangelization lies the suspicion that the Church no longer teaches the necessity of Christian faith for salvation. Did not Vatican II discard the ancient axiom "Outside the Church no salvation"? To be accurate, it reaffirmed the axiom, adding explanations that had become common in theology and papal teaching since the sixteenth century. All who are in a position to recognize the divine authority of Christ and the necessity of the Church have a serious obligation to become Catholics and remain in the Church. The Catholic Church, since it is heir to the fullness of God's revelation and possesses the full complement of the means of grace conferred by Christ on his Church, offers valuable helps for salvation. While profiting from these helps, Church members also have greater responsibilities, since much is required of those to whom much is given. Among the responsibilities is that of sharing the faith. Evangelization, therefore, is not superfluous.

Persons who are not in a position to recognize the necessity of believing in Christ and joining the Church may be saved, but only if they are positively related to Christ and the Church. Divine grace, which is offered to all, gives them the possibility of orienting themselves to Christ and the Church, so that when the gospel is credibly proclaimed to them they will accept it. If they do not hear the gospel, they can be saved through their spiritual orientation toward it, provided that they earnestly strive, with God's help, to do good and avoid evil.

Non-Christian religions, to the extent that they contain elements of goodness and truth, may help their adherents on the road to salvation, but to the extent that these religions are marked by sin and error they may actually pose obstacles. To assess the sound and unsound elements in any given religion would require a specialized study that only a few experts are qualified to undertake.

Judaism has a unique status among the world religions, since it rests on a series of revelations and historical deeds that Christians recognize as truly coming from God and as preparatory to the redemptive revelation given in Christ. While wishing that Jews may come to recognize Jesus as their promised Messiah, Christians rejoice in the rich patrimony that believing Jews already possess, in solidarity with the saints of ancient Israel. Christianity never ceases to profit from cordial dialogue with Jews in whom the faith of Abraham, Isaac, and Jacob still lives. Jews and Christians, while they differ on matters of great importance, are brothers and sisters having Abraham as their common father in the faith — a faith that Christians interpret as pointing forward to Jesus Christ. Jewish-Christian relations have at times been poisoned by acts of violence and persecution, especially those inflicted by Christians upon Jews throughout many centuries. The demand today is for repentance and reconciliation.

The realization that some people may be saved without explicit Christian faith should not diminish our zeal for spreading the gospel, which is necessary both for the Church itself and for the peoples to whom the gospel is proclaimed. The Church has a built-in drive to achieve its own catholicity by implanting itself in every culture and welcoming into its membership men and women of every nation, race, language, and social status.

Those who are evangelized likewise stand to gain. How could we justifiably withhold the message of the gospel and the means of grace available in the Church from anyone who is disposed to accept them? Neither individuals nor societies can rise to their true stature without knowing him who is "the way, and the truth, and the life" (Jn 14:6). As we shall see in Chapter 10, society itself is debased when human existence is not brought into proper relationship with God. The Christian conceptions of human dignity, freedom, and loving solidarity have an indispensable contribution to make in the fashioning of a civilization of love.

The New Evangelization

To counter the recent decline of missionary spirit, the Second Vatican Council and the recent popes have set forth a new program of evangelization, adapted to the present stage of history. John Paul II has succinctly called it "the new evangelization." It is not, of course, a completely new product. It retains the permanent characteristics of evangelization, but adjusts them to the current situation, which is in some ways unique. For example, we live in a time when the basic Christian message has already been preached in practically all countries, but still needs to be presented in more effective ways to elicit a firmer and more broadly shared response of faith. It is also characteristic of our time that some traditionally Christian and Catholic countries are falling back into what may be called a new paganism. To meet this complex situation, a new and more vigorous effort of evangelization is needed. Its features can be enumerated somewhat as follows.

1. Like all evangelization, the new evangelization is centered on the basic gospel message — that is to say, the Good News concerning the incarnation, death, and resurrection of the Son of God. The central truths of faith are those most intimately connected with the mystery of Christ; everything else is taught in conscious reference to the Paschal mystery of the Cross and Resurrection.

2. Evangelization, as seen in the present perspective, is not just a matter of intellectually persuading people of the truth. It calls for a transformation of individuals and socie-

ties in the light of the gospel. The gospel is a message that makes, and must make, a difference. It demands that those receiving it bring their attitudes and behavior, and not just their ideas, into conformity with Christ. The gospel needs to be proclaimed as a way of life and worship, not simply as a system of belief. Human existence, in all its aspects, needs to be permeated with the leaven of the gospel.

3. Evangelization is not directed to nonbelievers alone. It is directed to one and all. Every human being is and remains an object of evangelization. Three stages of evangelization may conveniently be distinguished.

- Primary evangelization is directed to beginners — those who have not yet heard the gospel effectively proclaimed. It takes place, for example, in the initial missionary proclamation in parts of the world where Christ is still relatively unknown and the Church is still a small minority. Such proclamation usually takes its inspiration from the kerygmatic sermons of Peter and Paul, as described in the early chapters of the Book of Acts.
- A second phase of evangelization consists in the continuing instruction and pastoral care of those who believe and are seeking to put their lives more fully under the influence of the gospel. It includes the education of the faithful to receive the sacraments as conscious and active participants. Catechesis, which presupposes some measure of evangelization, gives believers at least a rudimentary understanding of what they believe and prepares them to take their place within the corporate life and mission of the Church. But evangelization does not stop at this point, because even thoroughly instructed Christians still need help in submitting their whole lives to the power of the gospel.
- Finally, we must mention the reevangelization of those who have once believed but have fallen away or allowed their faith to grow cold. They stand in need of being helped to regain their Christian faith and practice. Younger members of formerly Christian countries, not having been

brought up in the faith, are in much the same status as their counterparts in unevangelized parts of the world. The primary evangelization of baptized Catholics is all too often neglected.

In the past, evangelization has generally been identified with the first of these three moments. But in recent years it has become clearer that the Church and all its members are in constant need of being more deeply evangelized. There are segments in the lives of every Christian that still need to be redeemed by confrontation with the mind of Christ.

4. Another point emphasized by Vatican II, and by the popes who have followed it, is that every Christian is called and expected to participate in the work of evangelization. Evangelization is not exclusively the task of bishops, priests, and "professionals." As noted above in our discussion of the sacraments (Chapter 6), all baptized and confirmed Christians are qualified to be witnesses to the gospel, even without any special appointment as preachers or teachers. All are in a position to bear witness to their faith not only by word but also, and perhaps especially, by example. Those appointed to pastoral office have the responsibility of motivating, directing, and monitoring the evangelization conducted in their communities.

5. A characteristic of our time, as noted by Vatican II, is a growing sense of the dignity of the individual person and of the rights of conscience. With this realization has come an increased sensitivity to the value of religious freedom. All too frequently in the past, people have been virtually compelled to profess the Christian faith in some form (whether Orthodox, Protestant, or Catholic) and sometimes even baptized against their will. Violence has been used against non-Christians or against Christians who did not belong to the established Church.

Today these coercive methods are generally, and rightly, repudiated. Most missionaries are very careful to make sure that new converts are acting with full freedom. Care is taken not to let their freedom be constricted by threats of punishment or hopes of reward. The freer the act of faith, the more solid and pleasing to God will it be.

6. In earlier centuries, missionaries tended to carry their own cultures with them. They did not clearly distinguish between the faith and its cultural expression. Converts were trained to express their newfound faith in the language and style of the missionaries, who came for the most part from Western Europe or, more recently, from North America. As a result, Christians in North and South America, Asia, and Africa tended to be highly Europeanized or at least Westernized, and in many cases they remained small foreign enclaves estranged from the culture of their nation.

Today, greater efforts are being made to find faithful expressions of the gospel that take account of the language, customs, and traditions of the people being evangelized. According to a popular expression, the faith has to be "inculturated" in the region. Generally speaking, it is a mistake to uproot converts from the culture they have inherited. By retaining their heritage, they can better appropriate the gospel; they can function more effectively in their ethnic countries and contribute more to the Church they are joining. With the passage of centuries, the Church has been progressively enriched by its contact with many cultures, and it stands to be further enriched by cultures to which it has been insufficiently exposed.

Inculturation, however, should not mean an unqualified acceptance of all features of the existing culture. Human cultures usually involve features that need to be purified and corrected in the light of the gospel. For example, one might think of practices such as sorcery, human sacrifice, slavery, sacred prostitution, the caste system, polygamy, and polyandry. Acknowledging the necessary tension or dialectic between the gospel and culture, the popes often speak of the dialogue between the two. They also call for the evangelization of cultures, asserting the necessity of regenerating cultures by an encounter with the gospel. Human cultures impoverish themselves when they exclude the riches of other traditions. Conversely, they always stand to benefit from opening themselves to the truth and goodness found in any cultural tradition, especially a tradition that has been leavened by Christian faith.

7. A final feature of the new evangelization is its readiness to take advantage of new modes of communication. The mass media, to be sure, cannot take the place of person-to-person contact, which can reach the individual's conscience in a way that evokes sincere adherence and commitment. Televangelists, it would seem, cannot achieve deep and lasting conversion without the follow-through provided by other factors, such as personal prayer, reading, and the support of a faith-community.

In comparison with some Protestant groups, the Catholic Church may have fallen somewhat behind in the proper use of the new media, which play such a crucial role in the formation of the younger generation. Electronic styles of communication are engendering a new mentality from which people accustomed to print culture are estranged. For the gospel message to be heard by this generation it must be translated, as far as possible, into images and language that can be disseminated by film, radio, television, and computers. Centers of evangelization should establish websites.

Ways must be found to authenticate reliable presentations of the gospel and to prevent people from being misled by factual errors and false interpretations. While it does not seem possible to regulate the new mass media by ecclesiastical censorship, systems of education and certification would seem to be important to protect the Christian message against deliberate or indeliberate distortions.

The challenges and the opportunities of the present age are enormous. We seem to be moving out of a comparatively static period when the world was divided like a checkerboard into regions that were Christian, Buddhist, Muslim, Orthodox, Protestant, and Catholic. People are entering and leaving all religious traditions at an accelerating rate. Religion, far from being in decline, is as vital as ever and more vital than usual. But no particular religion can afford to turn inward upon itself. To survive and prosper, it must radiate outward toward the world. Each generation has to be evangelized anew.

The faith has not been given to the Church as a private possession, but as a public trust to be passed on to others. To be a believer is also, by rights, to be called to be a witness, a herald of the faith. Jesus came into the world on a mission from his Father. The Holy Spirit is sent on a mission from the Father and the Son. The Church is essentially missionary. Its life is a participation in the twofold mission of the Word and the Spirit. The Word communicates the imperishable truth by which the Church lives. The Spirit impels the Church to proclaim its message with power and in so doing to expand.

Only within the present century has the Catholic Church grown decisively beyond its culturally Mediterranean matrix and become, in actual fact, a world Church. Evangelization, both Protestant and Catholic, is occurring with great success in many parts of the world. But for this process to continue, Catholics must overcome the pessimism and resignation found in some quarters today, especially in regions where Christianity has grown old. We need to learn from the younger churches and from persons who have come to the faith as adults. They can testify that the faith is still young. It has undying power to give meaning and purpose to the human project and to impart the deep interior joy that comes from communion with God. Having entered the new world of faith they cry out, with St. Augustine: "Late have I loved thee, O beauty ever ancient and ever new!" (*Confessions*, 10:27).

The Church and the Churches

In Chapter 4 we have considered unity as one of the four essential attributes of the Church. We have seen that while the Church is always one, it does not actualize its unity as much as might be desired because the members of the Church are sinful children of Adam, immersed in a world dominated by spirits other than the Spirit of Christ. Through the faults of Christians themselves, the family of Christ is divided into separate communions. These divisions call for repentance and for vigorous efforts to restore full communion. Thus unity is a task as well as a gift.

Ecumenical Principles

The task is not incidental or optional. It is a serious obligation, since Christ ardently willed that all his followers should be one. At the Last Supper he prayed that their visible unity might be a sign inducing the world to believe. What he prayed for must be possible, if not by human effort alone, at least with the assistance of the Holy Spirit.

In the twentieth century many Christian churches, including the Catholic Church, have been engaged in the ecumenical movement, a movement designed to overcome the divisions of the past and to restore the full visible unity willed by Christ for his Church. The Constitution of the World Council of Churches proclaims as the primary purpose of the Council to call the churches into visible unity in one faith and eucharistic fellowship. The Catholic Church at Vatican II officially entered the ecumenical movement and proposed a vision of unity that involved a common confession of faith, common celebration of divine worship, and fraternal harmony in one fellowship under the apostolic leadership of bishops in communion with the see of Peter. Although the Catholic Church is not a member of the World Council of Churches, it cooperates with many programs of the World Council and has been officially represented in the Faith and Order Commission since 1968.

The existing relations among Christian churches and ecclesial communities are complex. In varying degrees they are already in communion, insofar as the vast majority of their members are baptized believers in Jesus Christ. Many of them read the same Scriptures that Catholics do, recite the same ancient creeds, celebrate some or all of the same sacraments, and, needless to say, pray to the same Lord. Not a few are governed by bishops in the apostolic succession. All of these ecclesial elements bring them into a real, albeit incomplete, solidarity with Catholics.

Notwithstanding these basic similarities there are notable differences. Generally speaking, Catholics are alone in recognizing the pope as Peter's successor and as authoritatively commissioned to teach and govern the whole flock of Christ. In addition to this fundamental divergence in ecclesiology, there are other notable differences in doctrine and practice that continue to divide the churches from one another and from the Catholic Church.

This combination of unity and difference calls for a nuanced program of action. To the extent that we Christians are really, even though imperfectly, in communion with one another, we may and should engage in common witness, joint worship, and collaborative social action. But to the extent that our communion is incomplete, our common witness is necessarily impaired. Although we can generally confess our faith in the triune God and his incarnate Son, Jesus Christ, we cannot give united testimony concerning all points of faith. While we can join in many kinds of prayer and worship, including the annual Week of Prayer for Christian Unity, we are not yet in a position to celebrate a common Eucharist, the sacrament that expresses and sustains full ecclesial unity. While we can engage in many programs of common action, especially in service toward peace, justice, and the relief of misery, we must be cautious about programs that involve contested moral principles. We must be on guard not to be drawn into cooperation in evil, for example, by joining organizations that promote abortion and unacceptable methods of family planning.

Catholics have to be cautioned against two contrary errors. At one extreme, they might fall into the error of treating members of other churches as though they were not Christians or believers at all. This attitude fails to take account of the manifest faith and devotion to Christ displayed by these other Christians. It also overlooks the power of the Holy Spirit to use the Scriptures, prayer, and sacraments such as baptism as means of grace.

The argument is sometimes made that if others had the virtue of faith, they would assent to all that God has revealed, and hence to all the Catholic dogmas. But this argument is oversimplified. It ignores the difficulty that non-Catholics, lacking the guidance of the apostolic magisterium, may have in ascertaining the full content of revelation. Many of these Christians base their faith on the Scriptures and the early tradition of the Church. These sources may suffice, with God's grace, to elicit a genuine response of Christian faith on the part of persons who do not recognize the authority of the Catholic magisterium.

At the opposite extreme one finds Catholics who, in a misguided spirit of ecumenism, try to settle for a few fundamentals rather generally accepted by Christians, and treat the disputed points as mere matters of opinion. Even these minimalists disagree among themselves as to which doctrines are essential. In his days as an Anglican, John Henry Newman thought it possible to limit the "necessary articles" to the Scriptures, the early creeds, and the dogmatic decrees of the early councils, but he came to see that this compromise was illogical. It could be attacked on one side by Protestants who wanted to make Scripture alone the criterion and on the other side by Catholics who held that the dogmatic decisions of later councils and popes were also binding.

While Newman's views as an Anglican may have represented an acceptable Anglican position — a matter I have no intention of judging — he himself never thought that a Catholic could agree with him. When he became a Catholic, he repudiated his Anglican "middle way" as untenable. Without cutting off the process of legitimate development at some earlier point in time, he joyfully embraced the full faith of the Catholic Church as it had developed over the centuries. Only a false spirit of compromise could lead Christians to deny or conceal their differences for the sake of an apparent unity.

The different Christian churches, if they are faithful to their heritage, are bound to disagree, but they should not be complacent about their disagreements. Knowing that Christ wills that his disciples should live in visible unity and communion, they should strive to reach as much agreement as possible. To this end, many churches have commissioned theological experts of their tradition to participate in bilateral or multilateral dialogues. In these dialogues the parties are expected to give a frank presentation of the positions of their respective churches and to give an account of the reasons why they take the positions they do. But they are also expected to listen attentively and respectfully to the others, learning as much as they can from what they hear.

The ecumenical dialogues that have been conducted over

the years, especially since Vatican II, have yielded many valuable fruits. On some points the participants have determined that the supposed disagreements between their churches are chiefly a matter of terminology. Although they use different words, emphasizing different aspects of the revealed mysteries, the churches may be found not to disagree about the mysteries to which the words refer. On other points the dialogues have been able to discover that the churches' positions, while not identical, are complementary and compatible. On still other points the participants have seen that the positions taken in their own church have been one-sided and poorly grounded in the Christian sources. A more balanced position, based on a fresh reading of Scripture and of early tradition in a new and wider context, has paved the way for agreed statements. By steps such as these the partners in dialogue have found it possible to take forward steps, setting the churches on a path of convergence. While dialogue may not be capable of resolving all the disputed issues, it should be cherished as an excellent ecumenical resource.

In the ecumenism of the past decade, very fruitful use has been made of the category of communion (Latin *communio* or Greek *koinonia*). As we have noted in Chapter 5, this term designates the supernatural solidarity to which all human beings are called in Christ and the Holy Spirit. Insofar as communion affects the deepest recesses of the human person, it has an invisible aspect, but, as we have seen, it is never purely invisible. It comes to expression in the Church and is fostered through shared beliefs, common worship, and life together.

In terms of an ecclesiology of communion, one may say that the point of departure for ecumenical relations is the real though incomplete communion already existing among Christians. The method is to acknowledge that communion, to bring it to better expression, and utilize it for advancing toward closer communion. Full communion, as the goal of ecumenical endeavor, would require acceptance of the same professed faith, the same sacraments, and the same apostolic ministries. It would be crowned by participation in the same Eucharist.

The general principles of ecumenism set forth in the preceding pages have been stated at greater length by Vatican II in its Decree on Ecumenism, by John Paul II in his encyclical *Ut unum sint*, and by the Ecumenical Directory issued by the Pontifical Council for the Unity of Christians in 1993. These documents are normative and helpful for Catholics engaged in the ecumenical apostolate.

In all these documents it is recognized that the Catholic Church has very different relations with different groups of churches, including most prominently the Orthodox, the Anglican, the Lutheran, and the Reformed. A few words may now be said about each of these communions in particular.

Eastern Christianity

The Orthodox churches, most of which have their homes in Eastern Europe, are in many ways the closest to the Catholic Church. They have retained the faith as expressed in Holy Scripture and defined in the ancient councils. They have bishops duly ordained in the apostolic succession and validly administer all the sacraments recognized in the Catholic Church, including the Eucharist. Pope Paul VI said on more than one occasion that their communion with the Catholic Church is "almost complete."

This very proximity makes relations with these churches particularly delicate. In the Catholic understanding, they are already doing for their faithful much of what the Catholic Church does for its members. For the sake of salvation of souls, Catholics do not wish to diminish the influence of the Orthodox Church where it is still dominant or to upset the faith of its members. But Catholics cannot be satisfied with the communion that already exists because there are still serious disagreements in the area of doctrine and because Orthodox bishops are not in hierarchical communion with the see of Rome.

If these discrepancies could be overcome, full communion could be restored, to the advantage of both the Catholic and Orthodox communities. Without full incorporation into the Catholic communion of churches, the Orthodox churches and their members do not have access to all the blessings of the new covenant. While the hope is for full ecclesial reconciliation, this should not prevent individuals in the Orthodox tradition from moving into full communion with Rome for the sake of these additional blessings.

For a proper understanding of Catholic-Orthodox relations it has to be understood that the Catholic Church itself includes churches of different rites or disciplines. The Latin Church, which is by far the largest component, worships according to the Roman rite. In addition, the Catholic Church includes the Maronite Catholic Church, the Chaldean Catholic Church, the Syro-Malabar Catholic Church, the Armenian Catholic Church, the Coptic Catholic Church, the Melkite Catholic Church, the Ukrainian Catholic Church, the Ruthenian Catholic Church, the Romanian Catholic Church, and about a dozen others. This variety of ecclesial expressions shows forth the diversity in unity that characterizes the catholicity of the Church.

It would be a great impoverishment to suppress this variety of rites, even if such an act were a genuine possibility. Vatican II, in its Decree on the Eastern Catholic churches, affirmed their equality with the Latin Church and called upon them to rediscover their authentic traditions. It also affirmed that Eastern Catholics have a special vocation to foster ecumenical relations with the Orthodox. They have their own characteristic theological approaches, liturgical forms, spiritual and devotional traditions, and canonical rules. By their very existence, they anticipate the multiform unity that would presumably exist in a reunited Christianity. The Eastern Catholic churches should not be seen as obstacles to reunion, although they have sometimes been so depicted, but rather as bridge churches, interpreting the West to the East and the East to the West.

The theological differences between the Orthodox and

Roman Catholics are serious but probably not insuperable. With openness and good will on both sides, theological discussion could perhaps achieve the agreement needed for reunion.

The most debated doctrine is a very abstruse point in Trinitarian theology, relating to the procession of the Holy Spirit. The Orthodox generally hold that the Spirit proceeds from the Father alone; the Catholics, that the Spirit proceeds from the Father and the Son. As a compromise formulation, used by some of the Greek Fathers, it is often suggested that both churches can agree with the statement that the Spirit proceeds from the Father through the Son, or some similar formulation.

The other principal issue between Catholics and Orthodox has to do with Roman primacy. The Orthodox generally agree that the bishop of Rome holds a universal primacy in the Church and that nothing can be decreed for the universal Church without his approval. But they are not comfortable with the assertions of papal primacy and jurisdiction and papal infallibility that were adopted by the First Vatican Council in 1870.

In a possible future reunion, something akin to the relations between Rome and Constantinople in the first millennium could perhaps be reconstituted. The Orthodox would retain a certain measure of autonomy under the pope, whose dual capacity as universal primate and patriarch of the West would be more clearly recognized than is now the case. In the reunited Church the Orthodox could preserve their liturgical rites, their theological and spiritual traditions, and canonical integrity.

The most stubborn issues may be sociocultural rather than strictly theological. Tensions between Rome and Athens are very ancient, and go back to times before the dawn of the Christian era. The lack of communication during the Middle Ages (due partly to Muslim domination of the Eastern Mediterranean) and the unruly conduct of Frankish troops in the Crusades exacerbated the difficulties. At the present time, antagonism in the former Soviet Union is fueled by controversies about the return to the Catholic Church of buildings and properties that were taken from it by the Marxist government, especially in Ukraine, and handed over to the Orthodox. In addition, there are recurrent Orthodox complaints about "proselytization" by Catholics in formerly Orthodox territories.

Relations with the Orthodox are different in various countries. In the United States, for example, relations are generally cordial. This diversity of relationships is possible because of the relatively loose structure of the Orthodox communion. Orthodoxy is a communion of "autocephalous" churches that have their own patriarchs or metropolitans, while recognizing their subordination to the Ecumenical Patriarch of Constantinople. The power of the patriarch of Constantinople is moral rather than juridical. This fact, together with the endemic frictions among national churches, makes it difficult for the Orthodox to speak with a united voice.

When we speak of the separated churches of the East, we should not think only of the Orthodox Church, although it is the largest. Some Eastern churches broke away before the schism between Catholics and Orthodox in the Middle Ages. The Assyrian Church of the East has its origins in Nestorianism — a Christological heresy condemned by the Council of Ephesus in 431. A larger strand is represented by the Oriental Orthodox Churches, often called "non-Chalcedonian" because they never accepted the decisions of the Council of Chalcedon on the two natures of Christ in 451. This group of Eastern churches includes Armenians, Copts, Ethiopians, and Syrians, among others. Many of the Christological disputes that lay at the origin of these "non-Chalcedonian" churches have been resolved in ecumenical discussions, but their long estrangement from both Catholicism and Orthodoxy renders reunification difficult. The separate churches have developed in different ways.

Western Christianity

Turning to the West, we must take note of the unique status of the Anglican Communion, a worldwide body of churches that recognize the Archbishop of Canterbury as their primate. Anglicanism arose through a schism between Henry VIII and Rome, and shortly thereafter picked up certain Protestant elements from the continental Reformers. Anglican-Catholic relations have been troubled since the persecutions of the sixteenth century, in which both sides had their martyrs.

A turn for the better occurred with the meetings conducted between 1921 and 1926 at Malines, Belgium, under the presidency of Cardinal Désiré Mercier, in which efforts were made to draw up a program for reunion without absorption. After Vatican II, Pope Paul VI and Archbishop Michael Ramsey established the Anglican-Roman Catholic International Commission (ARCIC), with the mandate to clear the way to "a restoration of complete communion of faith and sacramental life." ARCIC has published a number of important agreed statements on topics such as the Eucharist, ministry, and authority in the Church.

While it is possible to achieve a high degree of consensus with certain Anglicans, it is difficult to produce consensus statements with which all Anglicans are content, since the Anglican communion includes Christians of very different theological orientations. The historic tendencies within Anglicanism are commonly referred to by such titles as "high church," "low church," and "broad church." There is no one voice that can speak for Anglicanism as a whole. The Archbishop of Canterbury has no jurisdiction or doctrinal authority over the communion as a whole.

Although the international dialogue and some of the national dialogues between Anglicans and Catholics seemed to be progressing well in the first decade after Vatican II, rising hopes for the mutual recognition of ministries and sacraments were set back by the growing acceptance of women's ordination to the priesthood in Anglican churches since the early 1970s. This step tended to align the Anglican communion with mainline Protestantism and distance it from Catholic, Orthodox, and conservative Evangelical churches.

A third major constituency with which Catholics have to deal is Lutheranism, which itself includes a number of churches, the majority of which belong to the Lutheran World Federation. In Germany, in the United States, and on the world level, very successful theological dialogues have been held, achieving something close to full agreement on baptism, ordained ministry, the Eucharist, and justification. The Joint Declaration on Justification signed at Augsburg on October 31, 1999, shows that one of the major causes of the split in the sixteenth century has been mended through patient dialogue. While theological differences between Lutherans and Catholics remain even with respect to justification, these particular differences are not considered to be so grave as to be, of themselves, church-dividing. Needless to say, substantial agreement on this one doctrine leaves many other points untouched. Although it does not suffice to reestablish full communion between the churches, the agreement on the basic doctrine of justification is a very hopeful sign.

Since Vatican II, the Catholic Church has been in dialogue with many other mainline Protestant churches, including the Reformed and the Methodist. These dialogues have been less strictly theological than those with the Orthodox, the Anglicans, and the Lutherans, but they have helped to establish mutual understanding, cooperation, and good will, thus minimizing the scandal of division.

Because the Baptist and Pentecostal churches do not have the kind of organization that lends itself to formal dialogue on the national and world levels, contacts between these churches and the Catholic Church have been more sporadic. Many members of these bodies take a negative attitude toward ecumenism and regard the Catholic Church as less than Christian. Nevertheless there has been a Pentecostal-Roman Catholic Dialogue on the international level, in which some charismatic Pentecostals have participated. There have also been some "conversations" between Southern Baptists and Roman Catholics on various levels.

The fastest-growing component of Protestantism in recent years has been a movement commonly known as "evangelicalism." It may be described as a loose association of Protestants who belong to a variety of traditions, including Reformed, Anglican, Methodist, Pentecostal, and Baptist. They tend to insist strongly on the doctrine of salvation by faith alone and to accept the sole authority of Scripture as the written word of God. They are suspicious of ecumenism as represented by the World Council of Churches and in many cases are antagonistic toward Roman Catholicism. Notwithstanding these obstacles, it has been possible since 1977 to arrange a series of successful conferences between theologians and missiologists associated with the World Evangelical Fellowship and colleagues appointed by the Holy See. In the United States an initiative known as "Evangelicals and Catholics Together" has published several significant statements of agreement on basic Christian truths such as the authority of the Bible, the Apostles' Creed, salvation through faith in Christ, and religious freedom. It is hoped that these and similar statements will foster greater cooperation between Catholics and Evangelicals on social issues, such as religious freedom and the defense of human life, and that they will reduce unhealthy competition and "sheep stealing" in missionary work.

A Final Reflection

Against the dark background of misunderstanding, mutual ignorance, and hostility in recent centuries, the ecumenical progress of the twentieth century is highly gratifying. The wars and violent persecution of Christians by other Christians are no longer the order of the day. Christ's followers increasingly rejoice in the beliefs and practices they share in common, including the Scriptures, the articles of the creed, the Ten Commandments, and much else besides.

Personal friendships growing out of ecumenical contacts have established new bonds across denominational frontiers. Catholics are edified to observe how other Christians, although they lack some of the sources of grace and sanctity available in the Catholic fold, exhibit an admirable spirit of faith, piety, and moral probity. They gratefully acknowledge that their partners in dialogue belong to the new world of faith and enlarge that world by their loyal service to the gospel.

As we enter the third millennium of the Christian era, we cannot help but remember that the second millennium, by introducing sad divisions, has greatly weakened the influence of the faith and inhibited the missionary apostolate. We can only hope that the Lord will give his followers the grace to turn away from past mistakes and embark on a course of reconciliation. The ecumenical movement, which began outside the Catholic Church but was irrevocably accepted by the Second Vatican Council, is still rich in promise. Provided that the churches who join in it continue to envisage the full visible unity of all Christ's disciples, ecumenism may bring added splendor to the new world of faith.

Moral and Social Teaching

In Chapter 2 we spoke of the biddings of conscience, which in normal people commands the doing of what is good and forbids the doing of what is evil. These biddings are absolute in the sense that we are always bound by them and no one can exempt us from the obligation. But we often find it difficult to discern what in the concrete is morally good or bad. For this discernment, three things are required: reason, experience, and instruction. In most societies a considerable degree of consensus is achieved about the nature of moral obligations. The Ten Commandments, while marked by certain specifically Israelite features, embody principles that have been rather generally recognized by civilized peoples as arising from the very nature of things. In that sense, the Ten Commandments may be said to be grounded in the natural law.

Morality and Religion

The Jews of the Old Testament were acutely conscious of the inseparability between morality and religion. God, they believed, would not accept the worship and sacrifices of people who violated their moral obligations and failed to repent. The prophets strongly insisted that religion requires the practice of justice and mercy, especially toward the poor and the afflicted.

Jesus emphatically reaffirmed this link between morality and religion. To enter into the Kingdom, he asserted, it is not enough to say "Lord, Lord," but it is required to do the Father's will (Mt 7:21). When people asked him about what was necessary for salvation, he pointed to the need to obey the Ten Commandments as a prerequisite for any further pursuit of perfection (Mt 19:18-19). What truly defiles a person, he said on another occasion, is evil thoughts, murder, adultery, fornication, theft, false witness, and slander (Mt 15:19). Before offering our gift at the altar we must first be reconciled with anyone we may have offended (Mt 5:24). In his scenario of the Last Judgment, Jesus made the performance of works of mercy the criterion by which the Son of Man will assign people to final blessedness or damnation (Mt 25:31-46).

Jesus saw the commandments to love God and to love one's neighbor as supremely important and mutually inseparable (Mt 22:37-40). In going freely to his death for the sake of our salvation he gave an extreme example of unselfish love, which served as the basis of a new commandment: his disciples should love one another as he had loved them (Jn 15:9, 12). Paul praised *agape* (charity), that exalted form of love that purely seeks the good of others. He taught that without it, no good works would have any value (1 Cor 13:1-3). These teachings on love, while in no way contrary to the Ten Commandments and the Mosaic Law, hold up a higher standard of generosity and self-sacrifice, and thus give an element of "newness" to Christian morality.

Although love is the animating principle of gospel morality, interior dispositions are not by themselves sufficient. Paul and other New Testament authors are as insistent as Jesus was on the observance of the commandments. They propose long catalogues of sins that exclude from the Kingdom of God — sexual misconduct, theft, robbery, drunkenness, and the like (1 Cor 6:10; cf. Gal 5:21). They also insist that in the judgment all of us will be rewarded according to our works (Rom 2:6; 1 Cor 3:8; Rev 22:12). It is impossible, therefore, to drive a wedge between Christian religion and moral conduct. The Church, with its responsibility to guide people on the way to salvation, is conscious of its mandate to teach the principles of natural morality.

Christian Social Teaching

The individualistic climate of our culture induces people to regard religion as a purely private matter, possibly important for the salvation of individual souls but of doubtful value for the right ordering of society, which is rather the concern of the state. But the Church is convinced that there is a moral dimension to political decisions that it has a right and duty to point out. While respecting religious freedom, the Church exhorts all people to look to Christ as the Lord who alone can heal and reconcile everything in heaven and on earth. Societies in which his help is sought through prayer, study, and sacramental worship will be blessed.

The political implications of the gospel did not come to the fore in the preaching of Jesus. The New Testament gives no hint that he saw himself as a social reformer. He disappointed the expectations of some of his followers by failing to take up the cause of national liberation against the Roman oppressors. Although he showed great love and compassion for the poor, he never incited them to seize the goods of the rich. His concern was to summon rich and poor alike to prepare for the imminent arrival of the Kingdom of God.

In the early centuries, when Christianity was a small and oppressed minority, the social teaching of the Church was as yet undeveloped. But after the conversion of the Empire, great theologians such as Augustine, Thomas Aquinas, and their followers, began to work out the elements of a Catholic theory of the state and of law, developed in dialogue with the political philosophies of antiquity. Only in the twentieth century has the magisterium of the Church authoritatively set forth the principles of Catholic social teaching. They may be found in papal encyclicals and in the teaching of Vatican II, especially its Declaration on Religious Freedom and its Pastoral Constitution on the Church in the Modern World. Recognizing that the secular state must administer to the needs of all citizens, regardless of their religious affiliation, the Church seeks to enunciate moral principles that are accessible to nonbelievers through the natural light of reason. Many of these pastoral documents are addressed not to Catholics alone but to all men and women of good will.

In its authoritative social teaching the Church does not seek to set forth a specifically Christian theory of politics, economics, or sociology. These disciplines involve technical questions that fall within the competence of specialists, and lie beyond the scope of the Church's magisterium. Still less does the Church claim the competence to govern secular society, which falls within the scope of the "things that are Caesar's" (Mt 22:21).

The Dignity of the Person

At the foundation of Christian morality lies the dignity of the human person. Even without the benefit of biblical revelation, many nonreligious thinkers regard the dignity of the person as practically self-evident, since it is obvious that persons, being endowed with intelligence and free will, are superior to mere things. Christians believe that human beings were made in the image of God (Gen 1:26-27) and, when fallen, were redeemed by the blood of Christ. Since all human persons have this dignity, they enjoy a fundamental equality.

From the intrinsic dignity of the human person flow certain human rights. The United States Declaration of Independence speaks of the "unalienable rights" to life, liberty, and the pursuit of happiness. Since the eighteenth century, human rights have been proclaimed in many national constitutions and international treaties. They are strongly asserted in documents of the United Nations, such as the Universal Declaration of Human Rights of 1948.

Recognizing as it does that human life is sacred, the Catholic Church has made itself a leading advocate of the "gospel of life." The Church defends the sacredness of human life as a gift from God that no one has the right to infringe. Life is to be protected from the moment of conception to natural death. Abortion and euthanasia, therefore, are ruled out. Suicide in its various forms is an assault on the sacredness of life and on the rights of God, the Lord and giver of life. While strongly insisting on the moral inviolability of innocent human life, Catholic social teaching does not deny the possibility that the right to life may be limited by certain misdeeds.

One such case is legitimate defense. People have a right to defend themselves and others against unjust aggression, provided that proportionate means are used. In cases of true necessity this may lead to the death of the aggressor. The responsible cause for the resulting death in such cases is the aggressor rather than the defendant.

Led by great theologians such as Augustine and Thomas Aquinas, the Church developed over the centuries a doctrine of just war, approving of the use of force under certain conditions for defense against foreign aggressors, provided that every peaceful means had been tried and failed. This traditional teaching has not lost its validity, but the applications are difficult under conditions where massive weapons of destruction are used, with the resulting death of many innocent civilians. Well-informed Catholics may differ in their judgment about particular cases.

The question of capital punishment invites similar discussion. In principle the state has the right to inflict the death penalty on dangerous criminals both to punish them and to protect society against them, but under contemporary conditions in advanced societies, it appears that other punishments are adequate to achieve the ends and are to be preferred as more consonant with the dignity of the human person. In the

United States the bishops have for a variety of reasons spoken out strongly against the death penalty.

The dignity of the human person gives rise to many rights in addition to the fundamental right to life itself. Some of the more basic rights are indirectly recognized in the Ten Commandments. When it forbids people to murder, commit adultery, steal, bear false witness, and the like, the Decalogue is indirectly affirming the rights to life, the integrity of marriage, private property, truthfulness, and the preservation of one's good name. Twentieth-century declarations from the United Nations and from Catholic Church authorities frequently mention rights such as those to education, work, a decent family wage, leisure, health care, freedom of speech, freedom of assembly, and freedom of the press. Rights such as these are flexible in the sense that their implementation varies considerably according to the conditions of society. A technologically advanced society such as our own, in times of peace, should be able to provide for these rights in a relatively generous measure.

Freedom and Subsidiarity

A second principle of Catholic social teaching, closely connected with human dignity, is that of personal freedom. Made as we are in the image of God, we have been endowed by our Creator with a capacity for self-determination. By freely following the judgments of reason, we are intended to assume a measure of responsibility for our moral and spiritual progress.

In current popular thinking, the concept of freedom is often distorted. It is understood to mean a mere lack of determination, permitting people to do whatever they please. It is often supposed that by entering into firm commitments, such as a religious or priestly vocation or marriage, we limit and impair our freedom. People are therefore urged to go through life unattached, as "rolling stones" guided by passing whims rather than firm convictions. Such lives quickly become empty and meaningless, and sometimes end up in suicidal despair.

According to the biblical and Catholic understanding, freedom is given to us in order that we may willingly embrace the true and the good. If we reject the known good, we fall prey to our lower appetites and instincts, enslave ourselves to selfish desires, and diminish our own freedom. But when we make sacrifices for the sake of adhering to what is right, we expand the zone of our own freedom. A deliberate and permanent commitment to a Christlike way of life is a very lofty exercise of freedom. In a sense, the martyrs are the freest persons on earth because they cannot be manipulated by fear of death or hope of earthly reward. They are prepared to renounce limited and ephemeral satisfactions for the sake of the good that is pure and abiding.

Some measure of human freedom belongs to every normal human being, but our freedom is restricted by our lower instincts and habits. The grace of Christ liberates us and gives us that greater measure of freedom which St. Paul describes as "the glorious liberty of the children of God" (Rom 8:21). In the Gospel of John, Jesus is quoted as saying, "The truth will make you free" (Jn 8:32). Since Jesus also tells us, "I am . . . the truth" (Jn 14:6), it is correct to say, with Paul, that Jesus has made us free (Gal 5:1).

The Church's high esteem for freedom has fed into Catholic social teaching ever since the time of Leo XIII, who wrote a major encyclical on freedom (*Libertas praestantissimum*, 1888). Increasingly since that time, the Church has encouraged democratic styles of government and denounced dictatorships and totalitarian regimes. Vatican II taught that political systems in which the citizens participate freely in the choice of their leaders are most consonant with human dignity (GS 75). The same Council accepted the principle of religious freedom, developed from earlier theological roots, and indicated some ways in which it could be applied to contemporary pluralistic societies. These social principles follow from the realization that God wants us to act freely in accepting the salutary truths of the gospel. He does not redeem us against our will.

John Paul II, following this tradition, strongly emphasizes the value of human freedom in the political and economic fields. He has words of praise for the free society, free enterprise, the free market, and free trade, but he also points out that the freedom to pursue social and economic goals is always limited by the obligation to respect the rights of others who are affected by our activity. Where the market economy is driven by selfishness and greed, it becomes an oppressive instrument by which the rich and powerful can trample on the rights and freedoms of the poor.

The slavery system, which had been accepted in most societies of the ancient world, was initially tolerated by Christians, who indeed had no opportunity to change it. But from the beginning Christianity alleviated the severity of slavery by insisting that slaves were to be treated with loving respect, as persons made in the image of God, even as brothers and sisters in the Lord. Eventually it was recognized that slavery in itself was immoral because it was opposed to the inherent freedom and dignity of the person and to the fundamental equality of all human beings.

As a corollary of freedom we may here mention a third principle, that of subsidiarity, which forbids higher governmental agencies from performing tasks that can be adequately handled by lower agencies or by private initiatives. The state must not be allowed to suffocate the freedom of individuals, families, and intermediate voluntary associations to do what lies within their competence. The role of the state with regard to education, culture, and the economy is a strictly subsidiary one. It sets the rules by which local initiatives can be coordinated for the sake of the common good, and intervenes only to fulfill needs that other agencies cannot supply. Catholic social teaching tends to be critical of the welfare state, in which personal initiative is crushed and inefficiency and corruption all too often abound.

Solidarity

In addition to the principles of human dignity, freedom, and subsidiarity I would add a fourth: solidarity. The virtue of solidarity has been defined by John Paul II as "a firm and persevering determination to commit oneself to the common good: that is to say, to the good of all and each individual, because we are all really responsible for all" (SRS 38).

Solidarity may be practiced on a variety of levels, within the family, the neighborhood, the city, or the state. Christianity, professing a kind of universal humanism, demands respect for all human beings, including those who seem to be the least important. On the basis that human beings constitute a single extended family descended from the same first parents and redeemed by Jesus Christ as the "new Adam," Catholic social teaching calls for universal solidarity among all races, peoples, and national states.

Solidarity calls for justice to all, but is not satisfied with the demands of justice. Human society cannot be successfully organized on the basis of rights alone. In the good society, justice needs to motivated and supplemented by love. In the absence of love, human relations will be plagued by hostility, recrimination, and endless litigation. In some cases people may at length obtain what they can prove they have a right to receive, but it will be given grudgingly, rather than freely. In love, we freely do good to others, regardless of their just deserts.

Solidarity gets us beyond the practice of dealing with others at arm's length, granting them only so much as strict justice requires. It inclines us to help others when they are in need and to share with them what we have to give. Seeking to be all-inclusive, the virtue of solidarity goes out in a particular way to the poor and the marginalized, who are not in a position to help themselves. The "preferential option for the poor," as it is called, is not a matter of privileging them over the rich but of speaking up for those who are voiceless.

In the teaching of Christ, love and mercy are not mere counsels; they are strict requirements. As we have received mercy, we are obliged to show mercy and forgiveness to others, including those who have offended us. Unless we are merciful we cannot expect God to treat us with mercy.

Pope Pius XII chose as his motto the words *Opus iustitiae pax* ("Peace is the fruit of justice"). Without denying this, John Paul II proposes that it might be better in our day to say *Opus solidaritatis pax* ("Peace is the fruit of solidarity," SRS 39). War, he points out, is usually the result of serious grievances, in which people feel that their rights are denied or their possibilities of self-advancement by peaceful means are cut off (CA 52). But reconciliation among nations cannot be achieved on the principle "An eye for an eye and a tooth for a tooth." If all insist on their supposed rights, and demand reparation for every evil they have suffered, tensions will never abate. In the end, forgiveness must be extended and accepted (DM 14).

Catholic social teaching can never cease to condemn the prejudices and ideologies of sexism, classism, racism, and nationalism as contrary to the teaching of Christ. It has consistently called for a limitation of national sovereignty and for the establishment of international authorities to deal responsibly with international problems such as the arms race, international trade, and the destruction of the environment. The Catholic concept of solidarity takes on new relevance with the increasing globalization of the economy. It calls for cordial relations within the "family of nations."

The Environment

In the past fifty years or so, the Church, like many other agencies concerned with public policy, has expressed increasing concern for the preservation of the environment. It is true that according to the Book of Genesis human beings have been given a certain dominion over the rest of creation. They have a right to transform nature by their industry and make use of its resources according to their needs. But this does not give them a license to pollute the earth, the air, the sea, to deface the beauty of creation, or to waste its resources that are intended for the benefit of all. The world has been given to us not only to be used but also to be cherished and contemplated. We have the responsibility to make the world what the

Second Vatican Council calls "a dwelling worthy of the whole human family" (GS 57).

While the hierarchy in its official teaching offers moral guidance regarding sociopolitical questions, it leaves its members free to reach their own decisions on concrete matters in which loyalty to the gospel does not manifestly call for a particular position. According to Vatican II and many subsequent instructions, the lay faithful are primarily responsible to make the gospel present in the world of marriage and the family and in those of politics, economics, diplomacy, medicine, culture, sports, and the like. It is up to them to carry the gospel into the home, the workplace, and the public square.

The Kingdom of God

In their programs for social action, Christians should constantly align their priorities with the gospel message, which tells us that nothing that happens to us in this life is ultimate. The Kingdom of God will be the work of God himself; it cannot be achieved by unaided human effort. Eternal life, which is the thing that matters most, is not promised to those who have been well fed, well housed, or well clad. The Church's main emphasis, like that of Jesus, should be on spiritual renewal. Without personal conversion the best social order will not succeed, and with such conversion even a badly ordered society can provide a measure of comfort and blessing.

The Church is called to be the herald and the sign of the reign of the blessed in the eternal Kingdom. It seeks to form on earth a communion of grace and love as described above, in Chapter 5. In that communion the members will treat one another as fellow members of Christ's body, which indeed they are.

While seeking to spread its salutary doctrine as widely as possible, the Church knows that much of its teaching will be seen as impractical by people who do not accept the radicalism of the gospel. For men and women committed to live by that radical vision, the Church can offer relatively small communities in which the members voluntarily dedicate themselves to live according to the ideals of the gospel. The members of these communities will be content with poverty rather than riches, self-denial rather than self-indulgence, meekness rather than self-assertion, humility rather than pride, and service toward others rather than self-service. Such communities, as contrast societies, will proclaim the gospel more eloquently by what they are than by what they say. They will be signs of what human life, with God's grace, can be at its best.

The moral and social teaching of the Church is not a mere appendix to its teaching about God, Christ, and the Church. The theory and practice of Christianity are inseparably intertwined. Believing as it does in a God who gave his own Son for our redemption, the Church is driven by love and compassion. Inspired by their faith and their love of the Lord, Christians are impelled to imitate his obedience, his humility, and his generous love. While fully adhering to the natural law and the Ten Commandments, Christians are animated by the higher law of love. The new world of faith inevitably leads into a new way of life. In accepting the call to follow in the path of discipleship, we are conscious that we shall often fail, but we are consoled by the assurance that God's mercy is always available to us, provided that we sincerely repent and seek to do better with the help of grace.

The Life of the World to Come

Have we any solid grounds for hope? If so, what can we hope for? These questions have continually perplexed thoughtful persons. Speculating on the final results of human activity, some ancient sages depicted history as an endless repetition in which all human accomplishments would be periodically reduced to ashes, so that the process could begin again, setting the stage for a new dissolution. Without embracing rigidly cyclical theories, many modern philosophers of history have argued that every good initiative will ultimately fall prey to the forces of corruption and death. In the cold death of the universe nothing will remain of our efforts, however noble.

In contrast to these pessimistic thinkers, others have viewed evolution and history as an inevitable progress. We human beings are seen as the protagonists, moving from conquest to conquest as we break through all the barriers of nature, until at the end we have established a kind of earthly paradise. Our hope, in this view, would be for people of generations yet to come.

The idea of a paradise constructed within history by human effort is in fact a grandiose myth. It is hardly compatible with the known weakness and corruptibility of all material things, with the permanent openness of human freedom to new acts, and with the persistence of sin and evil. Even if the theory were true, it would be dangerous and destructive. Fanciful projections have more than once been used to justify the liquidation of whole populations to pave the way for some future Utopia. The inviolability of the person demands that the goal of existence be attainable by each individual.

Quite apart from these aberrations, a destiny in which I have no part could well be a matter of indifference to me. There would be nothing to prevent me from choosing my own gratification as the standard for my actions. An effective system of morality requires that each of us be accountable for our actions before God, who will render a just judgment.

Our Christian Hope

Christian revelation makes it clear that every individual man or woman has a personal destiny beyond the grave. The new world of faith and grace, which we have been describing in previous chapters, is not limited to this life. It is a first installment of eternal life, which even now presses in upon us.

Already on earth the Church enjoys a mysterious communion with the saints in glory. The "communion of the saints" binds this world and the next together. The saints on earth experience an interior peace and joy that are not of this creation. They feel themselves drawn to the world beyond, so much so that this world becomes for them almost like a prison, a place of exile. We who are believers can say with the Apostle Paul that our citizenship is not in this world; our true home lies elsewhere (Phil 3:20). We are made for something higher, to which our whole being reaches out.

Precisely at this point, however, our speech falters and

fails. When we try to describe the final outcome that gives meaning and purpose to our pilgrimage, we run up against a barrier. Our curiosity is frustrated. Human speculation reaches its limits, and even revelation gives little clarity.

In speaking of the life to come, Holy Scripture relies heavily on two modes of speech, metaphor and negation, using them in combination. In a wild profusion of images, it tells us of two possible outcomes. On the one hand, it speaks of a heavenly city with gates of pearl, streets paved with gold, and angels playing harps; on the other, it describes a realm of outer darkness with inextinguishable fires, sulphurous fumes, gnawing worms, and gnashing of teeth. Then, shifting to a mode of negation, it declares that final happiness will not consist in food and drink; that for the blessed there will be no marriage and taking in marriage, no tears, and no temple, no sun, no moon. According to Paul we cannot even begin to imagine the things that God has prepared for those who love him (1 Cor 2:9). Of his own mystical experiences he writes that he was taken up into the third heaven and saw things of which it is impossible to speak (2 Cor 12:4). The resources of human language are overtaxed. It is as if a man born blind were trying to imagine the colors in a mosaic at Ravenna. We who have eyes could not tell him what he was unable to see except by relying on analogues from some other field, such as music or the culinary arts.

Death, Judgment, Purgatory

The portal through which we pass to the other world is death. This passage is almost a repetition of leaving the mother's womb to be born into life on earth. The unbeliever within us tends to resist the unfamiliar and to cling to what we have grown accustomed to. This resistance is natural enough, but some who have had near-death experiences attest that there is nothing fearful about death. They look forward to it as a doorway to our true home. These threshold experiences may not tell us much about life after death, but they do seem to demonstrate that the spirit has a life not totally dependent on the body. Quite remarkably, people who report on having lived out of their bodies testify that they were conscious of themselves and others, and could see and hear, even when their bodies were inert and their physical organs had ceased to function.

Death is not something that just happens to us. It is an awakening to a new and richer life. Our final and perhaps most important act on earth is that of dying. While we should not presume that we will respond appropriately, the grace of that moment could be abundant. It could well provide our last and greatest opportunity to turn to God in love. The possibility that hardened sinners may undergo a deathbed conversion can never be ruled out, but sincere repentance at that moment cannot be taken as a sure thing. Generally speaking, people die as they have lived.

According to Catholic doctrine, confirmed by the speculation of wise thinkers and the traditions of many religions, the soul is spiritual and immortal. Death is the moment of truth. As our self-deception is stripped away, God will show us to ourselves as we really are — that is to say, as we are in his sight. Holy Scripture tells us that judgment then will be meted out and that we shall be judged on the basis of what we have done in this life (2 Cor 5:10). The time for meriting rewards and punishments will at that moment come to an end.

In some religions it is taught that the dead will be reincarnated and live many times over, until perhaps at the end they will qualify for blessedness. This is not the Christian view. Revelation teaches us that we shall have no life in the flesh but the present one. "It is appointed for men to die once, and after that comes judgment" (Heb 9:27).

Nothing impure or defiled will be able to enter the holy sanctuary where God dwells (Rev 21:27). If we die with sinful attachments and inclinations resulting from past sins, even repented and forgiven sins, we shall be in need of further purification before we can be wholly caught up in the embrace of God's love. The Catholic tradition speaks metaphorically of purgatory as a place of burning. Paul himself already spoke of some persons who would be saved "but only as through fire" (1 Cor 3:15). The "fire" of purgatory is not an instrument of torture. It is a purifying agent by which the dross is separated from the gold. Some have speculated that that fire is not really different from the love of God, which makes a painful entry into souls not entirely prepared for it, burning away all that resists it. If there is pain in purgatory, it is because we have set up fences against God's love.

Sometimes Christian piety has tried to measure the time in purgatory, but we must be on guard against the tricks our imagination can play on us. If there is anything corresponding to time in purgatory, it cannot be coordinated with cosmic or earthly time. It is not measured by the movement of the earth in its orbit about the sun. In the duration of purgatory, a single instant might be equivalent to a thousand years. People who suffer painful illnesses and deaths may anticipate on earth what they would otherwise have suffered in purgatory.

The souls in purgatory enjoy the deep satisfaction of knowing without any possibility of doubt that they are among the saved. In the depths of their being they are united with God in grace. They love God and are loved by him. They have no ground for fear because the beatific vision will unquestionably be theirs. They are no longer capable of sin.

Purgatory is of concern to the Church because the souls there are part of the Church's family. In the communion of saints, all the members carry one another's burdens. The Church and its members therefore pray and offer sacrifices, especially the sacrifice of the Mass, for the deceased. This practice has scriptural warrant. Judas Maccabeus ordered prayers and sin offerings to atone for the sins of the fallen soldiers upon whose bodies forbidden amulets were found. The biblical author calls it a "holy and pious thought" to pray for the dead that they may be delivered from unexpiated sin (2 Mac 12:39-45).

The Reality of Hell

Quite different will be the lot of those who are lost. They will experience the frustration of never being able to satisfy the deepest craving of our human nature, which is to be united to the all-perfect God. Damnation, in Latin, is a synonym for loss. The word itself tells us that the essential pain of hell is the penalty of loss (in Latin, *poena damni*). The damned will experience the agony of separation from God. All their past unrepented sins will stand up, as it were, to accuse them. They will be haunted by the memory of what they did to resist God's love and his grace. For this reason, they will not need devils with pitchforks to torment them. They will be a torment to themselves.

Here again, as with purgatory, we should not be overconfident of our capacities to foresee what the reality will be. The vivid rhetoric of Christian preaching should not be taken as a literal description of hell. Dante's great poem, the *Inferno*, functions chiefly as admonition to remind us that sin needs to be taken seriously. The punishments will be appropriate. Sin has terrible consequences that we can only try to imagine.

God should not be seen as a cruel tyrant inflicting vengeance on his enemies. He desires that everyone should be saved but does not force their wills. He respects our dignity so much that he allows us to decide against him, rejecting the advances of his love. For those who refuse God's grace to the end, hell is inevitable. It is not an arbitrary punishment but is, in a sense, self-inflicted. Those who go to hell would not be happy in heaven. Since they hate God, heaven itself would be a hell for them.

"Lord, will those who are saved be few?" This question, put so anxiously to Jesus, wells up incessantly in every human heart. Jesus, however, did not give a direct answer. Instead he gave a warning: "Strive to enter by the narrow door" (Lk 13:24). According to another version Jesus said: "Enter by the narrow gate; for the gate is wide and the way is easy, that leads to destruction, and those who enter by it are many. For the gate is narrow and the way is hard, that leads to life, and those who find it are few" (Mt 7:13-14). These words are the nearest thing we have to a prediction, but they are more hortatory than informative. The intent is evidently to motivate us to pursue the demanding path to sanctity. In point of fact we have no statistics about the numbers of the saved and the damned.

In the Latin West, most theologians from the time of Augustine until rather recently were of the opinion that the majority of the human race would be lost. But in recent years, with some support from certain passages in Paul and the tradition of the Greek Fathers, it has become rather common to suppose that the great majority are ultimately saved. Could we imagine that God would allow his work to become, on the whole, a failure? Is not his grace more powerful than the venom of sin, as Paul seems to indicate (cf. Rom 5:20)? Is it not promised that Christ will reconcile all things to himself (Col 1:20)? Relying on passages such as these, Hans Urs von Balthasar and some others have maintained that we have a right to hope (although not to assert) that all will be saved.

The reticence of Jesus and Holy Scripture on this point is perhaps designed for our good. It keeps us from both complacency and discouragement. The quest for holiness is not a competition in which we strive to get ahead of others so as to be in the highest percentile on some antecedently determined scale, like students being marked, as they say, on a curve. On the contrary, we can best assure our own salvation by praying and laboring for the salvation of others.

Since we do not know how many will be saved, we must remind ourselves that we could reject God's grace and consign ourselves to damnation. For everyone on earth, final loss is a real possibility. When we turn our backs on God, we have no claim on him for the grace of repentance and forgiveness. But our fear must be tempered by childlike confidence in the Father, who loves us so much that he has not spared his own Son. We have every reason to think that he will bring to completion the life that he has begun in us through faith and baptism. Trusting in the power of God's grace, we are obliged to hope for our own salvation and that of our loved ones. We have no authorization to declare that any individual, past or present, is among the damned. The Church, although it canonizes saints, never pronounces on the identity of the lost. It has never formally taught that any human being is in hell.

Heaven

In the creed we say nothing about damnation, but we do express our faith in life everlasting and in the resurrection of the dead. Life everlasting is not something for which we need to wait until the end of the world. It can be granted in its fullness immediately after death, as the Lord intimated when he said to the repentant thief on the cross, "Today you will be with me in Paradise" (Lk 23:43). As for the resurrection, it is reserved to the end of time, although the Blessed Virgin Mary, by way of exception, was assumed body and soul immediately after her death.

What does it mean for the blessed to be in Paradise? We ordinarily think of Paradise as a place, like Eden as described in Genesis; but heaven, at least until the end of the world, will not be a place in the ordinary sense of the word. Except for Jesus and Mary, there will not be, so far as we know, any risen bodies before the general resurrection. In some mysterious way that has been a subject matter of much theological speculation, the blessed will be able to be know and love in the "interim period" before the resurrection of their bodies.

What will the blessed experience? First of all, they will experience the presence of God. They will know him as they are known, through connaturality with him (1 Jn 3:1). Through faith here below we know God dimly, as reflected in the mirror of what is said about him, but in the life to come there will be no need for any reflection; we shall see God directly, face to face (1 Cor 13:12). There will be a kind of compenetration between the divine Mind and our own. We shall see God by the light that he himself is. "In thy light shall we see light," says the Psalmist (Ps 36:9, KJV).

Besides being a vision, heaven may also be regarded as

an inheritance — something that is bestowed upon faithful children when their time comes to receive it. In the beatitudes Jesus pictures it as a land that the righteous will inherit. But in the same context he says that it is a vision given to the pure of heart, food and drink given to those who hunger and thirst for righteousness, peace for the peacemakers, and other things besides (Mt 5:3-10).

Even this proliferation of metaphors falls short of the full panoply offered by the word of God. In many passages heaven is described as a kingdom, in which the saints rule forever in union with God. It is also depicted in the Letter to the Hebrews as a people at rest, celebrating a perpetual sabbath. In the Gospels and the Book of Revelation the final Kingdom is portrayed as a messianic banquet, a wedding feast, and a heavenly liturgy.

The Book of Revelation, at the very end of Scripture, sometimes describes the presence of God in terms reminiscent of the Jewish temple, and at other times as a new Jerusalem with gates of pearl and streets paved in gold as pure and clear as glass. The city will be illuminated no longer by the sun and the moon, but the Lamb, the risen Jesus, will be its light. The city will be filled with fruit-bearing trees, with roots irrigated by the river of life-giving water, representing the fecundity of the Holy Spirit.

This immense collection of metaphors is intended not to confuse us but to rid us of confusion. A limited selection of metaphors could give a one-sided and misleading impression. We need the combination of all to correct our misapprehensions. Each metaphor has its value and makes its own contribution. Heaven will contain everything positive in all of them. It will be food and wine, music and song, worship and rest, jewelry and light. Purified of every element of earthly limitation, these images converge toward a magnitude that lies beyond our present powers to imagine. The metaphors, understood spiritually, point our thinking in the right direction, like a compass guiding us toward a harbor that lies beyond the horizon.

It is difficult to say whether there will be change in heaven. God himself does not change, though the effects of his activity obviously do. To the extent that we participate in God's own life, we shall share in his eternity. But no finite spirit can exhaust the infinite. Even in the beatific vision our perception of the divine will fall short of the reality, leaving depths of the divinity still to be explored. Some theologians therefore believe that there will be movement in heaven, and that the saints in glory will go from delight to delight as they contemplate the immeasurable perfection of God.

According to the Catholic doctrine of the intercession of saints, the souls in heaven "hear" and respond to the prayers of those on earth. In so doing they would seem to undergo some change — by learning what is needed here below and by acting in response. St. Thérèse of Lisieux, recently recognized as a doctor of the Church, said before her death that she wished to spend her heaven doing good on earth.

Unlike hell, heaven cannot mean isolation; our happiness would not be complete unless it were shared. Eternal life will not be a solitary affair but one marked by mutuality and conviviality. This aspect is brought home to us in the images of the messianic banquet, the wedding feast, and the heavenly liturgy. Such imagery makes it evident that the saints will be aware of one another. They will share in one another's glory, as do the guests at the same banquet.

Salvation is offered to individuals, but only insofar as they are incorporated into the communion of the saints, who will blend their voices in a single hymn of praise (Rev 5:9). The bride par excellence is the Church, but individual persons join in the celebration insofar as they are in communion with the Church.

Revelation does not tell us very much about the "horizontal" or "social" aspect of eternal life. We are generally inclined to suppose that we shall find our loved ones again, so that parents and children, brothers and sisters, husbands and wives, will be eternally reunited. This may well be the case. But we should keep in mind the teaching of Jesus in response to the question of the Sadducees about the woman who had married seven men in succession. Whose husband, they ask, would be hers in the life to come? Jesus replies that their question is based on ignorance. "You are wrong, because you know neither the scriptures nor the power of God. For in the resurrection they neither marry nor are given in marriage, but are like angels in heaven" (Mt 22:29-30).

The implication seems to be that there will be no special relationships based on flesh and blood, and that family ties will no longer count. We shall be in a society in which all love one another with a love so great as to exclude particularity. People who did not know each other on earth, and even those who disliked one another, will be united in mutual love. We shall not love our relatives less than on this account, but even more, for we shall love them in God and God in them, just as we love God in all his other sons and daughters. In this sense, God will be "everything to every one" (1 Cor 15:28).

Many other questions can be asked about eternal life. Some people want to know whether they will be able to talk with their favorite saints. Others, less piously, ask whether there will be cats and dogs, whether they will have their favorite pet, whether there will be beefsteak and ice cream, and all sorts of other curious questions. The answer is, I suppose, the one that our Lord gave to the Sadducees: the question is based on ignorance. It is foolish to want to know everything about the world beyond, because the answers, even if they came, would be unintelligible to us. We know enough to desire everlasting life; and the rest need not concern us. Why should we not be willing to wait? We will find out when we get there, and that is soon enough.

Even for those who get to heaven, at least one change is still in store. The end of the world, when it comes, will involve a new condition for all the blessed. There will be "a new heaven and a new earth," as we are told by several passages in Scripture (Is 65:17, 66:22; 2 Pt 3:13; Rev 21:1). The entire cosmos will be gloriously transformed, and will thereafter glow with the glory of the divinity. St. Thérèse will no longer have to concern herself with doing good on earth; she and the other saints can repose in the beauty of God and of the consummated universe. With their risen bodies, the saints will be able to experience the delights of heaven in new ways.

The End of the World

The end of the world is associated with the return of Christ as "judge of the living and the dead." The general judgment, it would seem, consists in the public manifestation of all the consequences of virtue and sin. All will be seen by all. The whole tapestry of cosmic history will be unfurled before our eyes. Sin will appear in its full loathsomeness, together with all the ill effects it has brought about. It will become evident why God permitted things that we imagine he ought to have prevented.

Christ will at this point appear in glory, clothed with the power of the Father. This second coming will be unlike the first one, when he came in humility, in the form of a slave. Now he will appear to all eyes, even to the eyes of those without faith, as he truly is: the Son of God incarnate.

As part of the glorious transformation, there will be a resurrection of the dead. The paradigm is the resurrection of Jesus, whose body, lying in the tomb, was vivified by his glorified soul on Easter morning. Paul, in First Corinthians, Chapter 15, explains that Christ's resurrection is the basis of our Christian hope. Our bodies, like seeds, must fall into the ground and die in order for them to rise in a new, imperishable condition.

On the basis of this and other biblical passages, the Church teaches that on the last day all will rise with the bodies that they had in this life. But there are different opinions about what is needed to make a body one's own. Some theologians, following the principles of Thomistic philosophy, hold that since matter receives its specification from the form, and since the spiritual soul is the form of the human body, my body consists of any matter that happens to be united to my soul. According to this opinion, no material continuity is needed between the body laid in the grave and that which rises at the end of time. A difficulty against this opinion is that it suggests reincarnation rather than true resurrection.

Theologians of a second school contend that there must be some material continuity like that which existed between the corpse of Jesus and his glorified body or that found between a seed and the plant that grows from it. This second opinion seems to be more consonant with the reverence that the Church pays to the bodies of the dead and to the relics of martyrs and other saints. Even though my body may have turned to dust and been dispersed, the risen body will be taken from its remains and not be a mere substitute for it. In the new earth every particle of matter will be most fittingly situated.

The appearances of the risen Christ indicate that the body in its heavenly condition will be exempt from the weaknesses that now afflict it. No longer governed by the laws of physics, it will be totally under the dominion of the spirit. Paul speaks of the risen body as imperishable, glorious, powerful, and spiritual (1 Cor 15:42-44). The classical theological tradition attributes to the glorified body the four gifts of impassibility, splendor, agility, and subtlety. Impassibility means immunity to physical pain and corruption. Splendor is the ability to shine with a glory like that of Jesus at the Transfiguration (Lk 9:29; cf. Wis 3:7 and Dan 12:3). Agility is the capacity to pass from place to place with the speed of thought. Subtlety enables these bodies to interpenetrate other material things and pass through them as Christ passed through the barred doors in the Upper Room of Jerusalem (Jn 20:19).

The doctrine of the resurrection sheds a new light on our self-understanding. It reminds us that it is unnatural for the soul to exist in separation from the body, since human beings are by nature incarnate spirits. Because the earthly bodies we now have are destined to be glorified, they are worthy of respect both before and after our death.

The end of the world, as we have it described for us in the Gospels, will be preceded by wars and persecutions, false prophecies and sacrileges. There will be unprecedented tribulations so great that unless the days were shortened, no human being could be saved. Love between human beings will grow cold, and faithful Christians will be hated by all nations. In his apocalyptic sermon, reported in all the Synoptic Gospels, Christ warned us of these things so that when they come we will not be shaken in our faith. Several New Testament texts refer to the future coming of the Antichrist, a powerful man of lawlessness who will oppose whatever bears the name of God until he himself is destroyed by the Lord (2 Thess 2:8; cf. 1 Jn 2:18-22). The Church may have to undergo collectively something corresponding to the Passion of Christ.

When Jesus made these predictions about the end-time, the disciples quite naturally asked him: "Tell us, when will this be, and what will be the sign of your coming and of the close of the age?" (Mt 24:3). Jesus, however, never indicated the date of the consummation. More than once he told the apostles that it was not for them to know the times and the moments that God had fixed by his own authority (Acts 1:7; cf. Mk 13:32-37).

On several occasions Jesus predicts that he will return like a thief, when least expected. Whenever he comes, it will not be late. Christ is always at hand, always ready to come; "he is near, at the very gates" (Mt 24:33), so that time does not so much approach him as run parallel to him. He is not nearer now than he was just after his Ascension. We must live as though he were to come within the hour, prepared to meet the Bridegroom when he returns. The posture of readiness is all-important.

For each of us personally the end will come with death, which likewise can occur suddenly and unpredictably. Let it not catch us unprepared. Death should not be seen any longer as an enemy, but as a friend. The sting of death has been overcome by Christ on the Cross. It has become, as stated above, the doorway to the fullness of life. Like Paul, we may licitly desire to depart and be with Christ (Phil 2:23-24).

For many of the prophets, the end of the world would be

a terrible and bitter day, a day of wrath and retribution. For Christ's faithful, however, it is a day of joy and exultation. At every sign of Christ's approach, they raise up their heads with the realization that their redemption is close at hand. The earliest liturgical prayer of which we have record is the Aramaic *Maranatha*, which means "Our Lord, come!" (1 Cor 16:22). In another form we have it in the concluding prayer of the Revelation of John: "Come, Lord Jesus!" (Rev 22:20). It resonates with the petition in the Lord's Prayer, "Thy Kingdom come." When we pray as Christians, we should do so with the realization that Christ, our Redeemer, has not abandoned us; we shall see him again, and when he returns he will bring his work of redemption to completion. "The Spirit and the Bride say, 'Come' " (Rev 22:17).

12 The New World and the Light of Faith

In previous chapters we have surveyed the contours of the new world of faith, beginning with the three-personed God, the author of all that faith adheres to, then examining his self-gift in Christ our Lord and the perpetuation of that gift in the Church with its hierarchical structures, its sacraments, its Scriptures, and its body of doctrine. We have also reflected on the ways in which Christians in the Catholic Church can best relate to other Christians, to other religions, and to the secular environment of home, business, and politics. Finally we have contemplated the shape of Christian hope regarding the resurrection of the dead and the life of the world to come. By way of a summary, it may be appropriate to draw together some reflections on the "new world of faith," which has been the title and the underlying theme of all that precedes.

Faith's New World

In the first place, the new world of faith is a world. It is a vast universe having its own laws, its own geography, its own chronology. In the Sermon on the Mount, and especially in the beatitudes, Jesus promulgated the charter of this new world. In his person and his career he exemplified the Kingdom in an unsurpassable way. The supreme law of Christ's Kingdom is the twofold precept of love for God and neighbor, the self-giving love that Paul extolled as the bond of all perfection (Col 3:14). Jesus imparted the radical character of his message by paradoxes. It is by losing our lives, he taught, that we find life (Mt 16:25); "it is more blessed to give than to receive" (Acts 20:35). The world disclosed to faith is immense. It opens up vistas that extend beyond the world of sense and into a realm not reached by telescopes and astronomical instruments, however powerful. Its landscape is marked by heights of ecstasy and mystical union and by depths of suffering and privation. Its population includes the living and the dead, saints and angels, and even, at its summit, the divine persons. The entire cosmos — insofar as it comes from God, stands under his dominion, and is destined to be transformed by God at the end of time — belongs to this new world. So do all men and women — not only Christian believers but also the vast multitudes who do not consciously enter this realm of grace; for they too are touched by God's love and called to respond to it.

This higher world has its own internal order and coherence. It is a cosmos, not a chaos, because Christian doctrine is an organic whole in which all the particular assertions refer to God himself or to creatures in relation to God. The truths of faith harmonize with, and cast light upon, one another. The world of faith has form and structure; it has a symmetry and variety capable of enchanting those who gaze upon it. That world is, in a sense, heliocentric, since its center is the Sun of Justice, Jesus Christ, who in his humanity reflects the glory of the eternal God and makes it shine in our hearts. All the redeemed are situated in relation to him and refract his light according to their own capacity, the munificence of God's gift, and the generosity of their response. The Blessed Virgin Mary is the supreme reflection, beautiful as the moon.

The world we have been describing has its own kind of

duration, different from earthly time. The redemptive act of Christ — his death and resurrection — constitutes the midpoint. Everything prior to the Incarnation points forward to Christ-event, and everything subsequent derives from it. The time line of salvation history, which originates with the promise of redemption extended to our first parents, was unrestricted before the time of Abraham. It achieved progressively greater intensity as God's election fell in a special way upon the descendants of Abraham, Isaac, and Jacob. After being narrowed down to a faithful remnant of Israel, the stream of revelatory and redemptive history was funneled, as it were, into a single jet at the point where the Son of God became man, recapitulating the earlier stages of the process in his own person. After Christ's death and resurrection, salvation history spreads out once again as the gospel is propagated to the whole world. The Good News meets with acceptance by some and rejection by others, but an inherent necessity dictates that it be proclaimed to all without distinction. Eventually the time of salvation history flows into eternity, as the faithful are taken up into everlasting blessedness, so that they may share in the inner life of God himself.

The world of faith is, in the second place, new. Far from being a mere extension of what we know from human philosophy, it brings us into a realm beyond the most extravagant dreams of philosophy. The rulers of this world never suspected what God was doing in Christ. "If they had, they would not have crucified the Lord of glory" (1 Cor 2:8). The very novelty of Christian faith makes it appear as weakness to the Jews and foolishness to the Greeks, but to those who are called, it is "the power of God and the wisdom of God" (1 Cor 1:24). To the eyes and ears of flesh and blood, it is a strange new world. It is alien to them, but only because they have already been alienated by sin.

This new world may be called a higher world, but it does not remain aloft, hovering over the realities of this earth. Because God created this world out of love, he cares for it and never leaves it unattended. Such is the extravagance of God's love for the world that he plunges into its very midst and descends to its depths by dying ignominiously on the Cross. By so doing, God the Creator claims the whole world by a new title, that of its Redeemer.

The old world of nature and the new world of grace exist concurrently. The protagonists of each are locked in a fearful duel, as the Church sings in the Easter sequence *Victimae paschali laudes:*

> *Mors et vita duello conflixere mirando:*
> *Dux vitae mortuus, regnat vivus.*
> When in strange and awful strife
> Met together death and life;
> The prince of life for us did die,
> And now he reigns in majesty.

The old world is subject to corruption. Eventually everything in it dies and recedes toward the formless state from which it had emerged. But the new world of faith is always new, because Christ says of himself: "Behold, I make all things new" (Rev 21:5). The Spirit of Christ, infused into it, renews the face of the earth (Ps 104:30). All of us who enter that world of grace live by new commandments (Jn 13:34), adhere to a new covenant (2 Cor 3:6), and eagerly await "new heavens and a new earth" (2 Pt 3:13; cf. Rev 21:1). We ourselves are a "new creation" (2 Cor 5:17). "Though our outer nature is wasting away, our inner nature is being renewed every day" as it tends toward the glory that is to come (2 Cor 4:16).

The forms and expressions of faith imbedded in history grow old. They must sometimes be changed like a vesture in order to show forth the unceasing novelty of faith itself, which is abreast of every time, pointing forward to the ultimate future that is the goal of all creation.

Faith and Its Growth

The new world is, finally, an arena of faith. We cannot even sketch it, still less enter it, unless we receive and accept

God's loving revelation. Reasoning may tell us why we ought to believe, but it cannot propel us into that higher realm. The contents of faith cannot be judged by the standards of the old world, which it challenges and, in part, rejects. Without reliance on the word of God, we are doomed to be strangers to the world of faith. To those who timidly cling to the old world with its familiar landmarks, the new world remains closed and inaccessible.

If we do enter that world, then, it is by making a fresh beginning, an act of faith whereby we acknowledge the relativity of merely human criteria and begin to contemplate reality through the eyes of Christ the Revealer. With the new eyes of faith we see all that we saw before, and we see it more clearly because it is lighted up by the lantern of faith, which suffices for believers until the bright day of eternity dawns in their hearts.

Faith, then, is a matter of opening ourselves to God as he speaks to us through his witnesses, especially Jesus Christ, the faithful witness (Rev 1:5), who gave his testimony before Pontius Pilate (1 Tim 6:13). Faith is a leap accomplished in trust and love. We renounce the right to judge by what we would have thought if we lacked the guidance of divine revelation. We accept new standards as well as new content. The standard is the Cross of Jesus Christ, by which we are crucified to the world and the world is crucified to us (Gal 6:14). What we counted as gain before we believed is henceforth reckoned as loss (Phil 3:7). All our values are transvalued.

From one point of view, faith is a kind of spiritual poverty. We turn to God as beggars, having nothing of our own on which to rely. In our very poverty we are made rich with the wealth bestowed on us by God. From another perspective, faith is a spiritual childhood. We come to Jesus as little children, asking him to teach us and clothe us with his wisdom. We adhere to him because in him God reveals the deep secrets that we need to know.

Faith is often, and rightly, called a submission to authority — that of the revealing God. God's authority is not just an extrinsic seal placed on something other than itself. It is the quality of the very person who speaks to us and comes in his word. God does not so much demand submission as gently evoke our assent by powerfully moving us from within. The Spirit of Christ enables us to adhere to his word with joy and ease.

Christ continues to make himself accessible today through the witnesses he has appointed and sent forth to speak in his name. The revelation is entrusted to the community of faith, and in accepting it we join that community. To become a believer is, in this perspective, a process of being socialized into a new community. We have to learn its language, familiarize ourselves with its symbols, and become at home with its furniture, its landmarks.

Catechesis, then, is a progressive induction into the community of faith. It is formation as well as information. Its goal is communion and intimacy with Jesus Christ. The result of the process is a kind of wisdom, especially if that word is understood as a translation of the Latin term *sapientia*, which connotes a taste (*sapor*) for the things of God. Thanks to the indwelling Spirit, the believer has an affinity with the divine and begins, as it were, to savor it. The theological tradition speaks in this connection of "connaturality" with the God of grace.

Prebaptismal catechesis terminates in two acts, which blend into one: the transmission of the creed and baptism. The candidate for baptism is expected to "render the creed" and in the course of making a profession of faith in the Father, the Son, and the Holy Spirit, is plunged three times into the waters of regeneration. The newly baptized put on white robes to signify the purity of their new life in Christ.

The transmission of the faith does not terminate with baptism. Having entered the new world by the passport of faith, the Christian uses faith as the compass by which to steer and as the motor by which to advance. The whole Christian life is a continual process of further immersion in faith, so that it more and more becomes the air we breathe and the instinctive rule of our thought and action.

We live in a day when the reception of faith by osmosis from the culture or by casual religious instruction can no longer be adequate. In many formerly Christian but now dechristianized countries, only a small percentage of the youth actually practice their faith. The mentality of the young is shaped for the most part, under peer pressure, by the secular culture of advertising, consumerism, and the mass media of communication.

Because the secular world is preponderantly antithetical to Christian revelation, faith requires for its growth an alternative environment, under the guidance of masters who are well grounded in Christian doctrine and exemplary in conduct. In his own day Jesus provided for this need by forming a group of disciples under his personal direction. He taught them to deny themselves, to take up their cross, and to submit to the baptism with which he himself was to be baptized. So too, in our day, the neophyte must willingly submit to education within the community of faith, under the supervision of tested leaders. This strenuous type of catechesis is needed not only for adult converts but for children baptized in infancy.

Prayer and worship are integral to formation in the faith. What we believe in theory and in principle must find expression in our converse with God. We speak to him as our loving Redeemer, thanking him for his gifts, entrusting ourselves to his protection, imploring his forgiveness, and consecrating ourselves to his honor and service. The official worship of the Church has an educative aspect; it is intended to shape the imagination and form the sentiments of believers so that they will better appreciate the teachings of faith and more faithfully adhere to Christian behavioral norms. By active participation in the Eucharist and other sacramental rites we obtain a certain experiential knowledge of the mysteries of faith. By Holy Communion the faithful "taste and see that the Lord is good" (Ps 34:8). They enter into deeper union with Christ the Head and with the whole mystical Body.

The validity of the gospel is confirmed by its fruits in those who embrace it. Their good works proclaim its truth. In another way it receives confirmation from the degeneration that follows from its rejection. The lives of unbelievers become directionless and erratic. Seeking freedom from God's law, they fall into a state of servitude. And like the Prodigal Son in the parable, they often begin to pine for the blessings of their Father's house, and perchance find their way back to it.

This experience of false freedom is replicated in the lives of whole nations. Some, tiring of the religion of the past, place their hopes in the sheer power of technology, which then begins to enslave its makers. On the global scale, our world is increasingly marked by division, violence, and fear. Whole continents are racked by misery and hover on the brink of despair. To all such people Christians can be heralds of hope if they live by the gospel and proclaim it. Assisted by the Lord of life, they can be apostles of human dignity and catalysts of renewal in forging a civilization of love.

The Dynamism of Faith

Authentic faith can never be sterile. Faith has a dynamism of its own whereby it takes hold of believers and transforms them into witnesses. The inchoative faith that moves believers to submit to instruction gives rise subsequently to an impulse to go forth and make disciples of others. Believers whose faith has matured through confirmation and catechesis are inwardly impelled to proclaim by word and example. The word of God within them presses insistently for expression. Recognizing this connection, religious education should aim not only to form and inform those being instructed but also to motivate them for the task of propagating the faith that is theirs. Catechesis can in this way serve as a link in the great chain of evangelization.

The transmission of faith requires in every generation an

active body of committed witnesses. Faith comes from hearing, and hearing from the word of Christ (Rom 10:17). Faith, then, is not possible without persons who testify. Believers submit to the word of Christ as it comes to them in the words of qualified human witnesses, those of the past enshrined in writing and those of today, some of whom we hear in person. If younger generations do not accept God's word, it is perhaps because no one has seriously challenged them to believe. We cannot expect them to believe unless the extraordinary Good News has been proposed to them with some of the urgency that moved the first witnesses to become martyrs. We must never allow ourselves to forget that the witness par excellence is the martyr.

In recent centuries the Church has been predominantly on the defensive, intent on shielding the faith of its members by staving off modern objections. To show that Christian doctrine is impervious to rational refutation is always possible and sometimes necessary, but much more is demanded for a firm and radiant faith. In the judgment of recent popes, the entire Church must today commit itself to the project of a new evangelization, new in ardor, methods, and expression.

The great mass of humanity lacks any strong conviction about the ultimate purpose of life on earth and any clear rationale for a viable moral and social order. Great masses of humanity groan under the yoke of oppression, violence, and grinding poverty. Christianity has come into the world not just to save a select few from the general conflagration but to save the world itself. We who are privileged to believe have an inalienable responsibility to spread the truth to all who sit in darkness and the shadow of death. According to the precept of Jesus, we are to be, as he himself was, the light of the world.

In our day we have many half-convinced or halfhearted Christians, reluctant to bear witness to their faith. They wait for inquirers to come to them and, when inquirers do come, all too often express their incompetence to give answers. Faith, to be sure, should be forced on no one. But it should be made as widely available as possible. If we have been brought into that life-giving communion with Christ that is the proper fruit of faith, we shall be intensely grateful; we shall be eager to understand what we believe and to share it with others. Indeed, we have no right to deny it to them.

The Excellence of Faith

Our readiness to spread the gospel cannot be a matter of perfunctory obedience. It must spring from appreciation of how much we have received and how much we have to give. In our faith we have a pledge and foretaste of the eternal blessedness of the saints. Its incomparable value may be summarized under three headings: truth, goodness, and beauty. These are the gifts that the human spirit ineluctably desires, and without which it starves and goes awry. In the new world of faith, all three are offered in abundance.

The wisdom of God, the eternal Word, has come into the midst of our human situation and has spoken the truth that can only come from God. Alone among the human family Jesus Christ could say, "I am . . . the truth" (Jn 14:6). He has bestowed the charism of truth upon his Church, "the pillar and the bulwark of the truth" (1 Tim 3:15). By his revelation we know whence we come and whither we are bound; we know also the Way, for he has disclosed it by his person, his action, and his words.

The mysteries of Christian faith open up a new world of truth, beyond the deepest speculations of the philosophers, but capable of sustaining the philosophic quest and bringing it to heights not otherwise attainable. Faith in no way diminishes the power of the mind to wonder, to reason, and to know. It stimulates our mind to go forward and supports its faltering steps in advancing toward the fullness of truth.

The spirit also thirsts for goodness. Whether we acknowledge it or not, the human heart is restless until it finds some absolute and total good to which it can give itself without restriction. God, who alone is that unlimited good, has given us in Christ a demonstration of goodness beyond the fondest dreams of the poets. Jesus represents in his life and teaching a spendthrift charity that is properly divine, as he sacrifices himself out of love for the sinners he came to redeem. He invites us to participate in his own divine goodness by obeying his new commandment of love and embracing the beatitudes. By following the "law of the gift" we experience that it is indeed more blessed to give than to receive. Our faith holds us to a far higher standard of conduct than we could achieve without it. The examples of Christ and the saints beckon us to rise to a new level of being and doing.

But neither truth nor goodness will fully satisfy us without beauty. Beauty has been aptly called the splendor of truth and the radiance of the good. Through beauty the intrinsic worth of that which is excellent in itself becomes a source of joy and delight. God as Creator is the author of all beauty and is himself more beautiful than all beautiful things. The glories of nature and of the starry skies point to him as their source. Those who discover God by ascending the ladder of creatures are moved to exclaim, as did Augustine, "Late have I loved thee, O beauty ever ancient and ever new!" (*Confessions*, 10:27).

In the Uncreated Word we have a perfect reflection of the Father's glory, and in the face of Jesus the incarnate Word the glory of God shines forth in unimaginable splendor (cf. 2 Cor 4:6). The Gospels do not tell us whether Jesus was handsome, but at least we know that in his Transfiguration, his face shone with a brilliance that anticipated the glory of his risen life. In his Passion, when his body was disfigured by the blows of his tormentors, his spiritual beauty shines more brilliantly than ever before. He glows with a new kind of beauty, that of generous love and unswerving fidelity — qualities that are distinctive to the new world of faith.

Throughout the centuries the story of God's self-manifestation in salvation history, and especially in the gospel story, has been celebrated in poetry, music, and the visual arts. The mosaics and icons of Eastern Christianity are so translucent to the divine that they seem to pulse with the breath of sanctity. In the monasteries and cathedrals of the West, the sufferings and death of Jesus, although lacking every trace of human prettiness, found expression in superlative works of art. The figure of the Crucified, with his grotesquely contorted limbs, can become, through the magic brushstrokes of a Grünewald, an object of arresting beauty, calling us to adoration and communion with the divine.

In his novel *The Idiot*, Fyodor Dostoyevsky has the hero proclaim, "Beauty will save the world." Pope John Paul II, among others, accepts that utterance as prophetic. Without beauty the truth would be unattractive, and goodness would seem harsh and forbidding. But truth and goodness enchant us when they are found to be beautiful. This combination is exquisitely realized in the new world of faith, in which God offers us a foretaste of his glory. In that world, not made by human hands, we can find our true and lasting home. Having entered the outer courts of God's dwelling by faith, we hope and pray that we may live forever in the sanctuary of his love.

> How lovely is thy dwelling place,
>   O Lord of hosts!
> My soul longs, yea, faints
>   for the courts of the Lord;
> my heart and flesh sing for joy
>   to the living God.
>
> — Ps 84:1-2

Index